Constructing Pakistan

Foundational Texts and the Rise of Muslim National Identity, 1857–1947

Constructing Pakistan

Foundational Texts and the Rise of
Muslim National Identity, 1857–1947

MASOOD ASHRAF RAJA

OXFORD
UNIVERSITY PRESS

OXFORD

UNIVERSITY PRESS

Great Clarendon Street, Oxford OX2 6DP

Oxford University Press is a department of the University of Oxford.
It furthers the University's objective of excellence in research, scholarship,
and education by publishing worldwide in

Oxford New York

Auckland Cape Town Dar es Salaam Hong Kong Karachi
Kuala Lumpur Madrid Melbourne Mexico City Nairobi
New Delhi Shanghai Taipei Toronto

with offices in

Argentina Austria Brazil Chile Czech Republic France Greece
Guatemala Hungary Italy Japan Poland Portugal Singapore
South Korea Switzerland Turkey Ukraine Vietnam

Oxford is a registered trade mark of Oxford University Press
in the UK and in certain other countries

© Oxford University Press 2010

The moral rights of the author have been asserted

First published 2010

ISBN 978-0-19-547811-2

Typeset in Adobe Garamond Pro
Printed in Pakistan by
Pixel Graphics, Karachi.
Published by
Ameena Saiyid, Oxford University Press
No. 38, Sector 15, Korangi Industrial Area, PO Box 8214
Karachi-74900, Pakistan.

For Jenny

Contents

Acknowledgements

This book owes its existence in the present form to the support of my family, friends, and well-wishers. I am grateful to all the members of my dissertation committee: Robin Goodman (Director), Hunt Hawkins, Amit Rai, Christopher Shinn, and Alec Hargreaves. Their constant guidance, support, insights and suggestions allowed me to finish the project and transform it into a book. I am also grateful to Naeem Raja, my brother, for his faith in me and for his uncanny ability to find primary texts not so readily available in the United States.

My thanks also to the Department of English, Kent State University for their support in the culminating phase of this project; I am especially indebted to Ron Corthell, the department chair, and my colleagues Mark Bracher and Babacar M'Baye for their material and intellectual support.

The early drafts of this book were written in Tallahassee, Florida where I had the absolute 'hall-pass' to work on this book, while my wife, Jenny, kept me supplied with hot cups of tea and took care of the day-to-day matters of our earthly existence. It is for this, and countless other reasons, that the book is dedicated to Jenny who has, in our five years together, shown me the true face of selfless love.

My thanks also to the editors of *International Journal of Asian Philosophical Association* and *Prose Studies* for allowing me to use some of my previously published work. I am also grateful to Jana Russ, David Murad, and Andrew Smith for their diligent proofreading of the final draft of the manuscript.

Finally, I am thankful to friends from all over the world whose presence in my life and whose trust in my abilities always encourages me to continue working towards a nuanced and compassionate representation of the cultures of the global periphery.

Introduction

It is with feelings of greatest happiness and emotion that I send you my greetings. 15 August is the birthday of the independent and sovereign state of Pakistan. It marks the fulfilment of the destiny of the Muslim nation which made great sacrifices in the past few years to have its homeland.... Muslims of India have shown to the world that they are a united nation, [and] their cause is just and righteous which cannot be denied. Let us, on this day, humbly thank God for His bounty and pray that we might be able to prove that we are worthy of it. (Mohammad Ali Jinnah).

In his inaugural speech, the founder and first head of state of Pakistan, Mohammad Ali Jinnah refers to a pre-existing Muslim nation that 'made great sacrifices' to achieve the nation-state of Pakistan. He also sees this transformation of the Muslim nation into a nation-state as a divine gift to the Muslims of India. Thus, according to Jinnah, the creation of Pakistan is the material representation of a divine blessing realised through human will. This realised dream relies heavily on the myth of 'having suffered together', for in defining national identities 'griefs are of more value than triumphs, for they impose duties, and require a common effort.' (Renan 19) Yet, Jinnah's inaugural speech is saturated with the silences that make his national claim possible. In most historical accounts of the Indian Subcontinent, the nation that Jinnah so gratefully mentions in his inaugural speech did not exist, nor was there any ethno-linguistic or, for that matter, religious imaginary of Pakistan (or a separate Muslim homeland) just thirty years before its birth. In fact, at the time of Partition, almost 'thirty-five million [Muslims] were left inside India, remarkably, the largest number of Muslims in a non-Muslim state' (Jalal 2). It is an established historical fact that Jinnah 'never quite abandoned his strategy of bringing about an eventual union of India on the basis of Pakistan and Hindustan' (Jalal 293). This implies that the actual creation of Pakistan can also be read only as a partial success of Jinnah's larger dream.[1] Until the time of partition of India (1947), even when the Indian Muslim national struggle was at its peak, Pakistan remained a novel, amorphous, and a loosely defined concept.[2] While this loose conceptual configuration of a Muslim nation played a strategic role in Jinnah's struggle for a separate nation-state, the very conceptual fluidity itself, it seems, has surfaced as the most enduring problem of legitimation for the postcolonial Pakistani nation-state.

Most metropolitan and Indian historians study the partition of India from two perspectives, namely, under the two registers of tragedy of partition and treachery of the British respectively. Thus, in the mainstream Indian historiography, the partition of India is represented as the last treacherous decision of a dying empire, while most British historians view the partition as a tragedy mostly caused by the intransigence of the All-India Muslim League leadership. Conversely, patriotic Pakistani departmental historians consider the creation of Pakistan as a triumph[3] of the Muslim struggle led by Muhammad Ali Jinnah.

By the mid-1940s, the concept of Pakistan had become a highly debated subject in newspapers, vernacular magazines and books.[4] An attempt has been made in this book to tackle the issue of an eventual partition from all angles of view, but keeping in mind the current political divisions as axiomatic. Thus, the main point emphasized in this book is that one needs to accept the Muslim demand for Pakistan as a fact, and then from there henceforth try to trace and analyse the points towards its support or refutation.

Postcolonial Pakistani departmental histories also create their own mythologies regarding this issue, and get into a rhetoric of the nation, tracing the rise of a separate Muslim identity as far back in history as imaginable.[5] For example, one of the most highly canonised textbooks on the Pakistan Movement, issued to the officers of all three major services of the Pakistani military, defends the need for a separate Muslim nation-state because the 'Muslims could not stoop to become their enemy's [Hindus] servants' (Munawwar 19). Yet another Pakistani historian asserts that Pakistan came into being the day 'the first Indian accepted Islam and recited *Kalima-e-Tawheed*,' (Fatehpuri 1).

All these historical explanations, however, fail to answer the most important question: How did the Muslims of India come to see themselves as a separate nation deserving a separate homeland? In my opinion, Indian Muslim nationalism, at least its proto-national tendencies, preceded Hindu or Gandhian nationalism of the All-India Congress.[6] By reading the textual history of Indian Muslim nationalism beyond the natural telos of Indian history, we can learn that the history of the nation and nation-state of Pakistan is inextricably linked with retrieving and foregrounding the cumulative acts of human will, leadership choices, and the politics of Muslim representation that narrowed it down to the final and terminal choice of a nation-state. To define the terms 'nation' or 'nationality', which I use as interchanging concepts, I am drawing on Karl Deutsch's functional definition of Nationality:

> Membership in a people essentially consists in wide complementarity of social communication. It consists in the ability to communicate more effectively, and over a wider range of subjects, with members of one large group than with outsiders. (27)

The functional aspect of this definition obviates the need to define nationality as an organic or objective state of being, and gives it a certain kind of dynamism that eventually may force a nation or nationality to strive for a nation-state of their own in competition with the groups that are considered 'outside the nation'. For the purposes of my discussion, the transition from the nation to nation-state involves a political process in which a certain national group employs its particular symbols, history, and socio-economic aspects of particularity to declare itself a sovereign political unit.

It will be safe to take the Indian Rebellion of 1857 against British rule as the most important climactic event and a temporal marker for the Muslims of India, for it prompted sudden political changes. To retrieve this rise of early Muslim exceptionalism, I will read the texts produced after the 1857 Rebellion as political responses to a changed political environment; hence my emphasis on politics instead of culture. I rely specifically on John Rapley's explanation of politics. For Rapley:

> Political regimes entail more than material accumulation and distribution. They always entail a cultural or spiritual dimension....Equally sudden change in the material conditions of people's existence will render prevailing ideas obsolete, initiating a period of cultural experimentation. *Politics is thus a conversation between governors and governed.* (Emphasis mine, 10).

For Rapley this 'conversation between the governors and governed' is instrumental in creating normative hegemonic structures for a new regime, but in his view the governed are not just passive recipients of the elite's hegemonic dispensations but participants to it. Even though culture and religion play a part in this process of elite-mass conversation, the process itself is inherently political. These are the particular connotations of the terms 'politics' and 'political' that I will be applying in my discussion of Indian Muslim nationalism.

While Indian nationalism in general has been a subject of many a scholarly treatise, Indian Muslim nationalism in its own particularity has not been treated in similar detail. Historical explanations of the rise of Indian nationalism can be broadly divided into two categories: the stimulus/response thesis group and its postcolonial critics. In fact, the very culturist bias of the post-colonial explanation of Indian nationalism is an attempt to refute the stimulus/response theory. This post-colonial intervention, however, focuses invariably on Indian nationalism within which the Muslim nationalism merits a discussion only under the general rubric of Indian communalism. Bruce McCully, one of the earliest proponents of the stimulus/response thesis, offers the following general explanation of the rise of Indian nationalism:[7]

> The native intelligentsia was bound together by ties of culture which set its members apart from their less fortunate fellow-countrymen; it was ambitious, capable, and highly articulate; its leaders knew what they wanted and did not hesitate to make their voices heard. In the native English and vernacular press they possessed an instrument of propaganda by means of which public opinion in India could be moulded in accordance with the views and interests of the educated community at large. (392).

This explanation of the rise of Indian nationalism presupposes the rise of national consciousness as a result of English education and the creation of a local intelligentsia. However, McCully mainly focuses on the rise of Hindu nationalism, and any references to Muslim nationalism are incidental and poorly researched. Surprisingly, this tendency to omit Muslim particularity even finds its way into late twentieth century challenges to the idea of 'downward filtration' and elite nationalism. Even in Gauri Viswanathan's brilliant work on the rise and function of English education, the idea of Indian nationalism remains uncomplicated by any suggestions of a particular Muslim sense of political identity.[8]

The downward filtration of Western ideas, the political role of the native intelligentsia, and the important role of party politics are also the normative modes of explaining the rise of Indian nationalism in the works of other theorists of nationalism. John Breuilly, for example, explains the politics of anticolonial nationalism by looking at the ideological aspects of political mobilisation: he divides anticolonial nationalist movements into three instructive phases: 'coordination, mobilization, and legitimation' (93). Looking at the level of maturity of political action, Breuilly opines:

As for Muslim nationalism, *it had barely taken shape by 1940*. In the elections of 1937, the Muslim League did very badly. On the other hand, the degree of Muslim involvement in Congress never recovered from the level it had reached during the Khilafat Movement of early 1920s. (Emphasis mine, 175).

This non-presence of Muslim nationalism, of course, only makes sense within the particular definition that Breuilly himself chooses for anti-colonial nationalism. In his words 'nationalism is, above and beyond else, about politics; and that politics is about power' (1). He further adds: 'The *only* starting point for a general understanding of nationalism is to take its form of politics seriously, and to study that politics in a way does justice to the complexity and variety of nationalisms whilst seeking to locate common patterns' (14). Hence, while Breuilly's shift from culture to politics is salutary, his elimination of texts or actions that may have not involved party politics but still contributed to Muslim exceptionalism is troubling. In Breuilly's self-described definition of nationalism, then, the politics of Muslim nationhood is clearly a latecomer, as it does not fit his tripartite model of anti-colonial politics practiced by organised political parties.

Conversely, Anthony D. Smith emphasises the role of ethnicity in defining a nation:

The position is rather more complicated in the Indian Subcontinent. Though the Punjabis provide the dominant ethnic community in Pakistan, there are a number of competing *ethnies*; yet Islam provides a rationale for wider territorial 'political culture' and the basis for a possible national identity, albeit heavily Punjabi in character. (113).

Smith is obviously attempting to fit Pakistani nationalism within his 'supra-ethnic Political Culture' (112) model, which can only be accomplished by extending the role of Punjabis as the major ethnic group. Even though Punjab is the most populous province of post-colonial Pakistan, Punjab's role in the Independence Movement was quite different. Historians of Indian Muslim nationalism are too preoccupied with matching a Muslim history to their own critical matrices that can only be studied in relative and reactionary terms.

In light of the above, I suggest that the history of Pakistani nationalism should be studied in two broad phases: (i) The post-rebellion articulation of Muslim exceptionalism; and (ii) The rise of the Pakistani nationalist movement after 1940. If read within this paradigm, Indian Muslim nationalism can be an independent subject of study, and Muslim nationalist consciousness serves as a precedent to Indian National Congress nationalism. As the post-1940s history of the Pakistan Movement has been recorded quite extensively in native and metropolitan scholarship, this work will mostly focus on the first phase of Indian Muslim nationalism; the articulation of Muslim particularity and exceptionalism.

Another important aim of this study is to de-privilege the culturalist explanations of the nation; and to foreground the importance of politics. If we study the rise of Muslim exceptionalism as political rather than cultural, then we can read the earlier loyalist tendencies of the Muslim elite as forms of resistance instead of as activities of an elite comprador group. The question of Muslim identity, I suggest, was always linked with the political realm. There could be no simple private public division of the Muslim idea of culture and selfhood, for Islam had always been considered a complete code of life that spanned the public and the private. It is this imperative to possess the political, that privileges politics, and not culture, as the main signifier of the post-1857 struggle of Indian Muslims. Hence, while social, religious and ethno-linguistic ideologies became part of the mobilizing discourse of the Muslim elite, the main problem was not cultural—for they had always had a thriving and distinct culture—but political, a question of survival under a national structure dominated by the British and native Hindus.

According to Anthony D. Smith, nationalist groups have three strategies for attaining a sense of ethnic history in defining the nation. His grouping includes the Neo-Traditionalists, the Assimilationists, and the Reformists. Out of these, Smith suggests, the Reformists negotiate the process of 'dual legitimation' the best by foregrounding the 'twin sources of authority in the modern world; that of the divine order and that of the scientific state' (119). Besides this 'dual legitimation', the secular Muslim reformers[9] had to make a dual negotiation; the one with the ruling powers and the other with the people. Therefore, all adoptions of the new order had to be in the name of the public and for the public good, a practice that I call the public imperative. These adoptions were also constantly attacked by *ulama* (religious scholars), the neo-traditionalist elite, who generally held more sway over the popular imagination. Because of this, it was imperative for the reformists to not only popularise western education but display tangible, material advantages of such westernisation. While religious leadership could postpone the outcome to the hereafter, the so-called reformists were doubly bound to Muslims to show the practical and material outcome of their relationship with the British. All aspects of upward mobility within the British system were consequently justified in the name of *Qaum*, or Muslim Nation. Thus the idea of a separate Muslim identity was built into the very rise of the new Muslim elite. The native elite, therefore, did not launch the nationalist movement simply in response to the impossibility of complete assimilation into a solely British system; it was an inherent part of their dual negotiation with the British and the Muslim public. Consequently, it is the so-called secular elite—or the professionals—who eventually became the chief exponents of a separate nationhood for Muslims.

The *ulama*[10] relied only on what A.D. Smith calls the 'divine alternative', and their way of reforming the Muslim society was to draw upon a pan-Islamic tradition deeply invested in Muslim history. The religious Muslim movements, therefore, existed in a dual temporal structure; they negotiated the present by retrieving the past. This past, however, was not merely cultural but political, in that the main concern of the *ulama* was not just to save the religion, but also to formulate a new language to describe the political realities in which Muslims had lost their political power, even the nominal rule of Bahadur Shah, that qualified India as the *Dar-ul-Islam* (abode of Islam). The *ulama*, therefore, had to decide in Islamic juridical terms whether or not India had become *Dar-ul-Harb* (abode of war). Traditionally, if a Muslim territory was taken over by a non-Muslim power, the land lapsed into *Dar-ul-Harb*, and Muslims were called upon to aid the inhabitants in their *jihad* (holy war) against the occupiers. The situation was further complicated because, as early as AD 1803, Shah Abdul Aziz, a leading *mujtahid*[11] of his time, had already given a *fatwa*[12] on the state of India:

> In this city (Delhi) the Imam-al-Muslimin wields no authority. The real power rests with the Christian officers. There is no check on them; and the promulgation of commands of *kufr* means that in administration and justice, in matters of law and order, in the trade, finance and collection of revenues— everywhere the '*kuffar*' (infidels) are in power. (Ziya-ul-Hassan Faruqi 2-3)

As the language of the *fatwa* indicates, the *ulama* were less concerned with direct threats to Islam than with having to define a political life in a land that had, at least technically, ceased to be the abode of Islam. This emphasis on the politics of Muslim life forced the *ulama* to develop a more pan-Islamic view of the nation, as opposed to a territorial definition of nationhood. If there was no local Muslim political authority left, the trust had to be placed in the trans-national symbols of Muslim authority.

As the main focus of my study is to retrieve the nationalist aspects of the loyalist school, only a few occasional references to the textual production of the *ulama*[13] shall be provided.

Overall, in both its manifestations, the Muslim negotiation of modernity under British rule was either mediated through the myths of a glorious past or by developing a conditional view of the present, one that incorporated acceptable modern knowledge into the Muslim reality. This tendency of the elite to work for the uplift of the *awam* (people) is what I have, for lack of a better term, called the 'public imperative'.

This public imperative is built into the very canonical teachings of Islam, and was further accentuated with the colonial encounter. The native Muslim elite always had to justify their existence through good deeds; the same cultural imperative now worked in forcing them to speak in the name of the people. Both the secular nationalist elite and the religious elite, therefore, structured their discourse around the concept of uplifting the people. This uplift included the social, moral, and especially, economic aspects of access to the new system of rewards and salaried income. At the very outset, then, because of its linkage with the people, the Muslim response to British power was public and political because of its linkage with the people. For this system to function, the people automatically had to be invoked even before the native elite moved into the British system of power. As the first duty of the native Muslim elite was to safeguard the interests of their own co-religionists, the idea of Muslim nationhood was therefore *a priori* inscribed in their upward movement. Hence, the Muslim approach to modern nationalism involved a combination of language of rights and betterment of the Muslim community.[14] The only difference in this process is that the nationalist elite functioned under the rubric of modernity, scientific inquiry, rationalism, and democracy, whereas the religious elite took it upon themselves to purify souls and give Muslims a sense of belonging to a distinctly Muslim political reality at their religious institutions.

The language of politics played an important role in Muslim interactions with the British. The religious leaders made their claims for the Muslim community in the language of a supranational Muslim universal, the *ummah*; they were, therefore, speaking from outside the language of colonial power. Their claims were based on a set of values and anxieties that spoke well to Muslim subjects but did not translate well for British officials, even though the latter did accommodate their demands within the juridical domain. The secular nationalist elite, however, developed a particular language of politics. For them, learning the language of the 'enlightenment' was the only way to reach British rationality, and their legitimacy depended upon the degree of fluidity and prestige accorded to them by the colonial system. Only then could they speak of the material advantages of flirting with the so-called infidel power. This development of a political language also involved developing the concept of the 'other' within the language of Muslim politics. Muslims had to be defined as different from their Hindu counterparts, their needs represented as special. The questions of quotas, separate electorates, and eventually a separate country were all based on a Muslim identity articulated in difference from the Hindus and not from the British.

The *ulama*, on the other hand, legitimated their power in the name of religion alone; for them the idea of religious survival was paramount. Hence, they also had to create an 'other' to justify their purist approach to the politics of difference. The reason they were so opposed to the idea of a separate nation-state was because Islam (for them) could not be confined to the boundaries of a territorial nation-state. Also, they believed that eventually, because of the power of their message, they would be able to convert enough Hindus to Islam to solve the problem of Muslim minority status. Surprisingly then, while secular leaders saw Muslim identity and its difference from Hindus fixed, the *ulama* saw Muslim identity as fluid and hoped to continue translating the religious difference through conversion.

Constructing Pakistan does not offer the history of Muslim nationhood as a unitary, progressive narrative, nor does it attempt to cover all possible texts produced during all stages of the nationalist movement. Rather, it focuses on some important and some hitherto forgotten texts dealing with the concept of Muslim nationhood in India under the Raj. The outcome, thus, is an amalgamation of literary, political, and religious texts all attempting to define a sense of Muslim exceptionalism, separateness, and eventually nationhood. Also, no attempt has been made in this study to proffer certain texts as more authentic than the ones previously written about. The emphasis on the whole has been on the textuality of history itself, and on the sociality of the texts and upon what Jenny Sharpe calls the 'truth-effects of fiction' (61-82). What comes out at the end is a disjointed narrative of Muslim nationhood, of which Pakistan was one isolated outcome but not necessarily the only outcome possible or desired.

My emphasis on textual reading stems from my disciplinary training: I am a literary critic and not a trained historian, and my approach to history is inherently mediated through an engagement with texts. The textual analysis of what I have termed the 'foundational texts' of Indian Muslim nationhood is informed by Edward Said's concept of 'worldliness'. In his book *The World, The Text, and the Critic*, Said explains the worldly nature of texts and textual analysis as follows:

> The point is that texts have ways of existing that even in their most rarefied form are always enmeshed in circumstance, time, place, and society—in short, they are in the world, and hence worldly. Whether a text is preserved or put aside for a period, whether it is on a library shelf or not, whether it is considered dangerous or not: these matters have to do with a text's being in the world, which is a more complicated matter than the private process of reading. The same implications are undoubtedly true of critics in their capacities as readers and writers in the world. (35)

Thus, obviously, in Said's view, the texts are never removed from the world in which they are produced, and similarly, neither is the reader or the critic. With this informed mode of interacting with the texts, one can, quite easily, assume that a critical rereading of texts, in itself, is also an attempt at highlighting the very worldliness of the texts, and the material conditions of their production as well as consumption as mediated through the worldliness of the reader and the critic. Thus, in my reading of these texts, the texts themselves serve as clues[15] in deciphering how and in what sense did the texts invoke, articulate, and posit an incipient sense of a Muslim national consciousness through their literal reorientations or through their affective value.

Literary production of the post-rebellion era, therefore, plays a major role in my analysis. Unlike the Bengali literature that needed authors like Bankimcandra Chatterji's vision 'to lead his people into a new era of speech and polity' (Lipner 19) by inaugurating a Bengali tradition of literature, the Muslim literature of the mid-nineteenth century did not need to be invented but reformed;[16] Urdu already possessed a vast corpus of literary texts, rules of language, and conventions of literary production. In post-rebellion India, as the British consolidated their control and established a new regime, the post-rebellion Urdu literature underwent an important change by adopting a utilitarian aesthetic and a loyalist emphasis. Hence, post-rebellion writers produced works—especially poetry—more pertinent to the changed state of Muslims. It is within this public imperative and language of loyalty to the British Order that the idea of Muslim particularity and exceptionalism is articulated. As the emergent British regime after the rebellion places Muslims either under suspicion, or completely outside its hegemonic project, the post-rebellion

Urdu literature, *a priori*, becomes intricately linked with the idea of Muslim rehabilitation within the New Order. This tendency to appease the power is certainly an elite practice but it is normalised in the name of the people. Hence, as will become obvious in the ensuing discussion, post-rebellion Urdu literature adapts to this new political imperative and literary production becomes more public. Since this public emphasis of literature is expressed in a language pertinent to the New Order, the public becomes inextricably linked to the political. It is in this process that the idea of Muslim particularity precedes the nationalistic politics of the Indian National Congress.

As stated earlier, the new regime topples the old Order and the vacuum so created is filled with those who are already either predisposed to form part of it, or who possess the material credentials to do so. The Hindu educated elite automatically find it easier to move into this vacuum.[17] For the Muslim elite, the new regime prompts the imperative to create a space within the New Order; they must prove their loyalty to the British, and to justify this move into what in popular terms is an infidel power this negotiation must be normalised in the interest of the people. Because of such an imperative, the immediate post-rebellion literary production must articulate itself from a loyalist stance, as well as in the name of the people. As the people happen to be Muslims, the new literature focuses prominently on the material conditions of Muslims, forcing the British to include the Muslims within the new hegemonic order. Appealing for inclusion into the New Order is not made under the rubric of individual freedom or the creation of an equal society, but rather as a particular concession to the Muslims who see themselves as poor and backwards. Hence, from the very start the Muslim problem is not a question of equal rights, but simply of the right to be included within the new political order. This inclusion can only materialise within the language of loyalty and not only in the language of rights, for rights, within a colonial structure, are not inalienable but granted.

Another aspect of Indian historiography that problematizes an understanding of Indian Muslim nationalism is the extreme focus on retrieving acts of native agency and instances of subaltern resistance within the language of native cultures. This extreme focus excludes pertinent colonial instructions or imperatives. A good example of this retrieval is Partha Chatterjee's work on cultural nationalism, which I will discuss in Chapter One. By locating the native acts of resistance within the private realm, Chatterjee is able to argue that Indian nationalism was expressed in terms of culture long before its political articulation. This cultural retrieval allows Chatterjee to challenge the downward filtration thesis, and bring to light a native subject capable of defining his/her own political destiny within the private realm. Another good undertaking that traces native acts of resistance and agency in non-elite groups are the works produced by the *Subaltern Studies Collective*. In an introductory essay in Volume 1 of the *Subaltern Studies,* Ranjit Guha describes this project as follows:

> Elite mobilization intended to be relatively more legalistic and constitutionalist in orientation, subaltern mobilization relatively more violent....Popular mobilization in the colonial period was realised in its most comprehensive form in peasant uprisings. However, in many historic instances involving large masses of the working people and petty bourgeoisie in the urban areas too the figure of mobilization derived directly from the paradigm of peasant insurgency. (4-5).

Intending to insert subaltern resistance into the fabric of elite history, most Subaltern Studies work focuses on recovering and recording such instances of peasant insurgency. There are very few such instances of Muslim insurgency that Subaltern Studies recovers from the post-1857 history, even though the north-western border of India maintained an active Muslim rebel camp for quite some time after the rebellion.[18] Emphasizing native resistance is yet another reason why the rise of Muslim national consciousness is traced to the 1940s, for most Muslim political acts until then do not qualify under the rubric of native agency or resistance. In fact, such an approach can easily turn out to be an indictment of the secular Muslim elite for their complicity with the British. I suggest that this post-1857 rebellion Muslim cultural production should be read in its own specificity, within the language of loyalty and the idea of Muslim backwardness in comparison to their Hindu counterparts. If the aim of such a Muslim–British negotiation is to ensure Muslim inclusion and change the relationship of dominance to one of hegemony, then the language of loyalty forms a kind of resistance. If read this way, one is able to see that the particular Muslim response to the post-rebellion British Order precedes the Bengali nationalist tendencies, and successfully articulates the Muslim exceptionalism and particularity under the new regime. This tendency to claim loyalty to the new regime starts as an individual project; several members of ousted Muslim nobility rehabilitate themselves through contractual and openly declared loyalty, which later matures into a more public method of presenting the Muslim condition to the British.

In Chapter 1, I read Mirza Asadullah Khan Ghalib's post-rebellion diary to illustrate the early phase of this particular Muslim condition. The Muslim political texts of that period develop an important concern with articulating the Muslim conditions immediately after the rebellion. I will discuss this point in Chapter 2 by juxtaposing works of Sir Sayyid Ahmad Khan and W.W. Hunter.

Indian Muslim nationalism was inherently ex-territorial, in the sense that it traced its history beyond Indian borders within the supranational concept of *ummah*. This ambivalent dual view of nationhood also complicated the articulation of Muslim particularity. As Muslim literature took a utilitarian turn in post-rebellion India, it also drew upon the transnational Muslim past to question the present and to articulate a future. In this effort, the rise of the Muslim *ummah* was traced not just in its religious sphere, but also in its modes of knowledge production. In the works of Muhammad Hussain Azad and Altaf Hussain Hali, the Muslim nation emerges in its Indian particularity, but with a supranational history and a need to acquire modern knowledge to make room within a new British regime. During this phase of literary production, writers no longer speak for themselves but speak in the name of the Muslim nation. In Chapter Three, I will discuss this important aspect of Muslim exceptionalism in the works of Azad and Hali.

Chapter 4 focuses on the early Urdu novel. Using two novels of the first Urdu novelist Nazeer Ahmad, I will discuss the development of the Muslim public sphere and the specific peculiarities of post-rebellion Muslim loyalism, while explaining the two modes of inclusion—the mundane and the heroic—into the British system.

Chapter 5 is an attempt to explain that the Muslim response to the raj was never monolithic, as the works of Shibli Naumani and Akbar Allahabadi, the two main critics of the loyalist Muslim politics, represent. This discussion will also highlight the importance of and the return to the Islamic tradition in the works of conventional Muslims, and their attempt at retrieving the Muslim subject of resistance.

Chapter 6 focuses exclusively on Muhammad Iqbal and his contribution to the Muslim critique of the West, as well as his articulation of Muslim nationhood. I continue my discussion of Iqbal, Mawdudi and other *ulama's* views on Muslim nationhood in Chapter 7, which is followed by a brief conclusion of my project.

To summarize, this book is an attempt to explain early Muslim responses to the post-rebellion British regime, the different points of view, and the idea of Muslim exceptionalism that takes shape in this process. I believe that the rise of Muslim politics of nation-state cannot be understood without paying due attention to the early rise of Muslim exceptionalism. This brief study, I hope, will convincingly state that Muslim nationalism started long before the 1940s, and that its articulation was a more complex process than what we are accustomed to find in traditional histories of Indian Muslim nationalism.

NOTES

1. Ayesha Jalal's main argument is about this failure of Jinnah's larger vision. For Jinnah's plan to succeed, he needed a strong centre that would accept a parity of parliament seats between the Muslim League and Congress, hence, ensuring a safeguard for the Muslim minority provinces while at the same time keeping the particularistic tendencies of the Muslim majority provinces in check. Jinnah was also opposed to the partition of Punjab and Bengal and had envisioned a secular Pakistani state that would safeguard the rights of its own minorities. These non-Muslim minorities were to be a safeguard, coupled with the strong centre, for the interests of the Muslim minorities inside Hindustan. Hence, in Jalal's view the Pakistan that came to be after the partition was the one that Jinnah had vehemently rejected in the early 1940s.

2. According to Ayesha Jalal, given Jinnah's precarious position of negotiating the intricate terrain of Hindu, British, and Muslim politics, it was in his best interest to leave the concept of Pakistan as loosely defined as possible.

3. Most Pakistani historians pose an idea of irreconcilable Hindu–Muslim differences and tend to suggest that Pakistan had come into existence in AD 712 when Muhammad Bin Qasim, leader of the Muslim expeditionary force sent by the Caliph Wahid, invaded Sindh and Multan, present day Pakistan.

4. Some major works of the time include: *The Meaning of Pakistan* by F.K. Khan Durrani; *Pakistan: A Nation*, by El Hamza; *India Divided*, by Rajendra Prasad; *Confederacy of India*, by A Punjabi; and *Pakistan or the Partition of India*, by B.R. Ambedkar.

5. Some such Urdu historical works include books by Subhan Rai Batalwi and Sheikh Muhammad Ikram.

6. I use the terms Hindu/Congress or Gandhian nationalism interchangeably as descriptive terms to differentiate it from Muslim nationalism. It is important to remember that Congress nationalism was never really only Hindu nationalism. In fact, until the very end the Indian National Congress had a sizeable number of Muslim elite and the Muslim population as its members.

7. McCully's discussion of the Indian nationalism, which he links with the rise of English education, primarily focuses on Hindu/Congress nationalism with some brief references to the rise of Muslim nationalism. Overall, his work is not much different from his successors who also focus mainly on the genesis of Indian nationalism.

8. One could, of course, argue that as both these authors are dealing with the period preceding the rise of the Indian National Congress, the Muslim politics cannot form an important part of this. It is, however, important to note that during this time, especially immediately after the 1857 rebellion, a large corpus of Muslim works articulating this particularity was being produced.

9. It is important to note that the secular Muslim reformers were not truly secular in the Western sense of the word. In fact, most of the early reformers were religious scholars,

but can be treated as secular reformers for their willingness to accept certain aspects of Western modernity.

10. For a good explanation of the *ulama's* contributions see Sayyid Tufail Ahmad's work.

11. A *mujtahid* is a religious scholar trained in the law of Islamic jurisprudence to give an opinion on the questions of Islamic law and *Shariah*. Shah Abdul Aziz is extremely important in Indian Islam because all major sects of Indian Islam revered him.

12. Unlike its common translation in English, a *fatwa* is not a verdict; it is an opinion by any leading *mujtahid* on an issue of Islamic law given sometimes in answers to personal questions, but often to questions of public interest. More than one scholar might give differing opinions about the same case. In such a situation the individual can choose the opinion that he or she must follow. Only a legitimate Muslim government can implement a public *fatwa*.

13. Two good works on the reform movements of the *ulama* are Barbara Metcalf's *Islamic Revival in British India* and Zia-ul-Hasan Faruqi's *The Deoband School and the Demand for Pakistan*.

14. This important difference between Indian nationalism and its liberal Western counterpart is discussed quite brilliantly by Bruce McCully (293).

15. Here I am drawing on Fredric Jameson's explanation of the Hermeneutical method of reading, a mode of reading in which the text itself serves as clue to reading the larger structures in which it was produced. For details see Fredric Jameson, *Postmodernism, or, The Cultural Logic of Late Capitalism*, pp. 8-10.

16. Almost all historians of Urdu literature trace the beginning of Urdu poetry to the extant works of Amir Khusrau (1253/54–1325). By the mid-nineteenth century Urdu literature had developed into a highly evolved form and boasted two schools of poetry: Delhi and Lucknow. For details about the history of the Urdu language and literature see Ali Jawad Zaidi.

17. According to Bruce McCully, 'in 1865–66 out of 1,578 students enrolled in colleges for general education, a survey revealed only 57 Mohammedans ... as compared with 1,426 Hindus and 95 others belonging to neither of the dominant communities' (179).

18. I touch upon this history of the rebel camp in my discussion of W.W. Hunter's work.

1

The Indian Rebellion of 1857 and Mirza Ghalib's Narrative of Survival[1]

The greatest poet of his time, Mirza Asadullah Khan Ghalib (1797–1869) was sixty-two years old at the time of the Indian Rebellion of 1857. Though associated with the court of Bahadur Shah Zafar, Ghalib was a pensioner of the East India Company until 1820, a privilege that he lost due to a family dispute.[2] Even before the rebellion began, Ghalib's loyalties, like so many other nobles of the waning Mughal era, were split between the Company and the ceremonial Mughal court. Ghalib's 'range of conscious interest included not merely the literary and intellectual circle of Delhi....It went beyond the [Mughal] court to the new British rulers' (Spear 40). Ghalib's views of the rebellion are, therefore, mediated through this dual identity: as a member of the Muslim nobility; and as a dependent of the East India Company. This chapter aims to read Ghalib's *Dastanbuuy: A Diary of the Indian Revolt of 1857* as a public document to trace one particular literary response to post-rebellion British Raj.

Dastanbuuy is the most neglected work of Ghalib. This is partially because the text—so openly pro-British—problematizes the popular perception of Ghalib as a candid and courageous Indian national poet.[3] In the words of one of his critics, *Dastanbuuy*, an account of the rebellion, is 'blatantly pro-British and ruthlessly condemnatory of the Revolt' (Varma 142). Ghalib, of course, himself a part of the aristocratic poetic tradition,[4] did not feel any empathy towards the sepoys who marched on Delhi: to expect this empathy with the people would be a little anachronistic, for as a poet he belonged to a culture where the boundaries between the *shurfaa* (the aristocracy) and *awam* (the people) were quite impermeable.[5] Muslim society had its own peculiar class system based on lineage, region, religious sect, and differences between rural and urban populations. B.R. Ambedkar[6] considers these divisions as a sort of a Muslim caste system in the subcontinent, and cites the Census of 1901 to explain these divisions of the Bengal Muslims:

The Mahomedans themselves recognise two main social divisions, (1) *Ashraf* or *Sharaf* and (2) *Ajlaf*. *Ashraf* means 'noble' and includes all undoubted descendants of foreigners and converts from high-caste Hindus. All other Mahomedans, including the occupational groups and all converts of lower ranks, are known by the contemptuous terms, '*Ajlaf*', 'wretches' or 'mean people': they are also called *Kamina* or *Itar*. (103)

Some of these categories certainly applied to Ghalib's Delhi as well and play a very important role in understanding Ghalib's view of the rebels. To Ghalib the rebels were from amongst the *ajlaf* and, therefore, a threat to the *shurfaa* community's interests.

Pavan K. Varma reads *Dastanbuuy* as a strategy of survival, since the British were 'ruthless in victory; the slightest suspicion was sufficient for a man to be hanged' (141). Varma also suggests that the book should not be read literally and that its purpose was 'to influence the powerful' (143). Varma goes on to locate a more honest and candid Ghalib in his letters, hence placing Ghalib's native loyalty within the private realm of letters. He also suggests that the 'more emphatic the pro-British sentiment of the *Dastanbuuy*, the more it is revealed to be what it was: an ingenious cover to hide Ghalib's real involvement in the Revolt' (151). Through this intricate analysis of the work, the critic ends up reaching an idealised posture of the native resistance: we must therefore retrieve Ghalib, as a subject of resistance, through a critical reflex in a work that is so openly pro-British. The translator of *Dastanbuy* warns us that, 'divorced from its historical context, it is easy to view the life of Ghalib with a spirit of condemnation or apology' (20), which means that we need to read Ghalib's diary differently. Farooqi, however, is still more concerned with the intricacies of the text itself rather than the process of its production. Within the postcolonial paradigm of retrieving acts of native agency, both these approaches to reading Ghalib are quite apt, and enable the critic to recover the resistant voice. However, the text can also be read differently by placing it within the particularity of a changing political order in which the Muslim poet is forced to face the new power through an expression of loyalty. Reading Ghalib's diary as a political text allows us to retrieve if not a resistant Ghalib, then a Ghalib who understands his own condition in its particularity, and attempts to speak to power within this political specificity.

Ghalib's *Dastanbu* is translated as *Dastanbuuy: A Diary of the Indian Revolt of 1857*. The word diary, however, is a misnomer, for it elicits a certain trained reader response. One expects the diary to be a private document, a text not part of the public archive but rather an account of the private. This association, therefore, leads one to expect a more candid account of the events, a more honest and maybe more apt rendering of the sufferings of the Indians and Muslims at the hands of the British. The diary automatically forms an important part of the historical corpus that Dipesh Chakrabarty terms 'History 2' (63). This tendency to recuperate resistance in the private realm is further intensified within the culturalist explanations of native Indian nationalism as theorised by Partha Chatterjee. In tracing the autonomy of the native subjects in imagining a separate national space under colonialism, Chatterjee divides the colonised space into two realms: 'the material and the spiritual' (6). He amplifies this argument as follows:

> The material is the domain of the 'outside', of the economy and of statecraft, of science and technology, a domain where the West had proved its superiority and the East had succumbed. In this domain, then, Western superiority had to be acknowledged and its accomplishments carefully studied and replicated. The spiritual, on the other hand, is an 'inner' domain bearing the 'essential' marks of cultural identity. The greater one's success in imitating Western skills in the material domain, therefore, the greater the need to preserve the distinctness of one's spiritual culture. This formula is, I think, a fundamental feature of anticolonial nationalism in Asia and Africa. (6)

For Chatterjee, then, it is in the private spiritual realm that the idea of native nationhood takes hold and hence, the rise of Indian nationalism can be traced to acts of native agency, instead of relying on the theory of downward filtration. Chatterjee also claims that the private realm was a sort of autonomous realm that kept the colonial power out of its domain (6). In such explanation, the private realm becomes the ultimate space for the expression of exclusive native agency, an agency unhindered by the politics of the public sphere. In the light of this, it is perplexing to find Ghalib, the so-called intellectual voice of his times, so militantly pro-British even within the private confines of a diary. A private archive, retrieved and inserted into the official rendering of history, has been the most potent critical weapon to unravel the departmental claims of colonial administration, but in *Dastanbuuy*, we must reverse the order, we must declare and prove beyond doubt, instead of suggesting not to read it literally, that it is instead a public document garbed within the language and nomenclature of the private. Thus, immediately after the rebellion, the main struggle for the Muslim elite was not to preserve the Muslim culture in the private, spiritual realm, but to forge a place within the new hegemonic order, and this movement, in my opinion, could only be facilitated through the language of loyalty.

Reading Ghalib's 'diary' as a (non)diary—a public document aimed at a specific audience, a 'conversation' with the new governing elite for his own personal interest, transforms the diary into a public document—'a political act' by which I mean that the writings were consciously aimed at influencing the dominant elite in order to gain material advantages within the new political order. For this reason, we must examine the very materiality of *Dastanbuuy*, the mode of its production, and the process of its publication. We need to read *Dastanbuuy* within its own context, and define a new way of reading that is self-reflexive and self-critical. We need especially to ensure that we do not read the texts of the periphery in order to correspond with the metropolitan critical agendas of retrieving hidden narratives of resistance.

There is, I suggest, no need to stretch our critical matrix to a point where we can bring it in acceptable alignment with the understanding of Ghalib by his readers and postcolonial critics. Reading the work as a political attempt at negotiating a rising political order itself obviates the necessity of defending Ghalib's loyalty to his own people. At the risk of lapsing into the intentional fallacy, we must retrieve, as far as possible, the declared intentions of the author about his own work, and then read the work accordingly. In other words, we must conduct what Edward Said elaborates as a democratic, humanistic reading, a kind of reading that reads Ghalib 'as if with the eyes of' Ghalib and attempts to 'understand each word, each metaphor, each sentence as something consciously chosen by' (62) Ghalib. According to Said, this mode of reading enables the critic to read a text within the material context of its production, and with due deference to the intentionality and worldliness of the author. To accomplish this, we must read *Dastanbuuy* not just in its broader historical context, which is covered by almost all Ghalib critics, but within the very specific context of its publication.

About the nature of changing regimes of power, John Rapley suggests that a 'sudden change in the material conditions of people's existence will render prevailing ideas obsolete, initiating a period of cultural experimentation' (10). It is also important to note that in Rapley's terms, almost all elite-popular relations are governed by the politics of material distribution, and the masses form alliances with the elite to best serve their economic interests. In the case of the Muslim elite of India, gaining a political voice in the newly changed system is inextricably linked with the question of Muslim economic interests. Ghalib inhabits this experimentation phase of changing political times. In Post-Rebellion Delhi, while the previous elite-people consensus has ended, the old elite is under suspicion and most of them are incriminated in various acts of revolt. As the British take control of Delhi and launch the post-rebellion reprisals, Muslims find themselves the special subject of harsh British treatment. This makes it imperative for the Muslim elite to create a space for themselves in the new emergent order. Written during this turbulent period, Ghalib's diary carries the impact of this new power structure and becomes an emblem of a new way of dealing with the British power: a mode of representation based on the language of loyalty.

Reading *Dastanbuuy* along with Ghalib's letters of the time informs us that *Dastanbuuy* was never intended to be a private account of the rebellion: it was rather a public text, specifically aimed at proving Ghalib's loyalty to the new dominant elite, and to make a case for the restoration of his pension. While the account of the rebellion, written in classical Persian, provides a proof of Ghalib's loyalty, the material text itself also serves as evidence of Ghalib's loyalty. By publishing *Dastanbuuy* in record time, Ghalib transforms himself from the status of a former Mughal court poet, to a poet whose pro-British works, available in the public record, speak of his loyalty to the new order. *Dastanbuuy*, therefore, is a piece of evidence placed in the public records by Ghalib to be used if he is tried for treason.

The most important evidence regarding Ghalib's approach to *Dastanbuuy* and its production is found in his letters[7] of 1858–9 to Munshi Hargopal Tafta, one of his students and friends. It is in these letters that I will first trace the itinerary of the material production of *Dastanbuuy*, and then progress to reading the actual text within the material circumstances of its production. *Dastanbuuy* emerges suddenly in a letter to Munshi Hargopal Tafta (17 August 1858):

> Now, listen to a project: I have written a fifteen-month account of the city [Delhi] and my own situation from 11 May 1857 to 1 July 1858. I have ensured that the prose is in classical Persian that excludes any Arabic words, including the poems cited within this work....There are no presses here; I have heard of one but their copywriter is not *Khushnawis*. Let me know if it can be printed in Agra. (282)

The words of the passage have more depth than meets the eye. In the first line, 'project' is a rough translation of the Persian word *am'r*. In the *Persian–Urdu Dictionary* this word is listed as two different words with different meanings. Both the words, however, are of Arabic derivation.

The first entry defines *am'r* as command or proclamation; and the second one implies a job or project. In technical terms *am'r* is also, both in Persian and Arabic, an imperative form of the verbs. I have translated *am'r* in the letter as *project*, for that is what Ghalib broaches in the ensuing lines, but the word's polysemy should not be easily elided, for Ghalib is also here instructing Tafta to begin a new project. The second accentuated word is *khushnawis* which literally means 'the one with a nice handwriting'. Thus, one major reason for Ghalib to publish his work in Agra is that Delhi's only press has a calligrapher who is not *khushnawis* enough. To understand the implications of this sentence one must first, briefly, understand the process of Urdu and Persian printing at that time. Until the modern typewriters made it possible to compose Urdu texts for printing, early Urdu printing was far more labour-intensive. A calligrapher—a *khushnawis*—first wrote the master copy, which was then sent to the artist for *taz'een* (decoration). The master-copy was then sent to the printer for large-scale production and circulation. The final outcome of the printed manuscript depended heavily on the talent of the calligrapher. Its true importance will be discussed later, but what needs to be stressed here is that the reason Ghalib desired for *Dastanbuuy* to be composed in Agra is because better calligraphers could be found there. This signifies that, somehow, the presentation of this particular work was probably more important than the work itself. What can clearly be understood here is that Ghalib has written a personal account of the rebellion but wishes it to be published in Agra which offers superior quality calligraphy.

In another letter dated 28 August 1858, Ghalib enquires from Tafta about 'five ornate copies' (284) that he had mentioned in a previous letter. This is not an odd thing, for most Urdu texts were traditionally published in two forms: a standard version for the public and a *munaqqash* (ornate) version for presentation to collectors and sponsors. One could construe from this that Ghalib intends to send at least five copies of his work either to his sponsors or to some other people of importance. His previous letter is even more telling now, for if he wants five ornate copies, then it is vital that he finds a better calligrapher and press. In another letter to Tafta written on an unspecified day in August 1858, Ghalib explains the reason for his haste:

> I understand your questions about the printing. You will understand it better when you see this work. The reason I want to get it published quickly is because I want to send one copy to Governor General Bahadur, and one copy through him to the Queen of England. This should give you a hint about the

style of its writing and the reason why publishers will not turn it down. (285-86)

This letter transforms this venture into something far more public in nature. But then, knowing that Ghalib was famous for sending his *Qasidas* to the British officials,[8] one might argue that there is nothing special about this instance of sending copies of his recent work to those in power. What we do know is that the five ornate copies are to be sent to all the major British functionaries in India including a copy for the Queen. Yet the desired haste for this printing is perplexing. Ghalib is also very particular about the authorial name that is printed on the published copies of the diary. He wants his official name—Mirza Asadullah Khan Bahadur Ghalib—to be inscribed on the book. In his words: 'administrators in Delhi know me by my nickname [Mirza Nausha] but from Calcutta to England, including ministers and the Queen's office, none knows me by this name' (288). So Ghalib is particular about which name to use, and wants it to be published under his official name, the name known to, and listed in English official records. In one other letter Ghalib also insists on adding a copyright notice at the end of each book. The book is eventually ready by 18 November 1858 and Ghalib receives the first batch of its standard print on that day.

On 20 November, he finally receives the seven (the number has increased) ornate and specially produced copies of the book. Ghalib writes to Tafta: 'I don't know how to praise these texts. The style is regal and the outlook like the sun' (303). These books, we learn, are being sent to 'the Governor General, the Queen and various secretaries of British administration' (303), and Ghalib, having completed the project, concludes his letter of 27 November by musing about 'what the Chief Commissioner and the Governor will say' (305) when they receive the book.

We learn some important facts from these letters: *Dastanbuuy* was most certainly written during the time of the rebellion; Ghalib was insistent upon the literary and the material quality of the work; the work was produced and distributed within approximately three months of its initiation; the ornate volumes were intended for all the major British functionaries, as well as the Queen; and Ghalib was aware that his official name must be used for an intended audience unfamiliar with the name by which his usual readers knew him. All this clearly suggests that Ghalib's diary was intended to be a highly deliberate public document written for a specifically British audience. As this act of writing corresponds to what

John Rapley considers 'a conversation between the governors and the governed' (10), it therefore becomes a political act, one aimed at a specific audience to affect their perception of the author.

Dastanbuuy may thus be read as a political document. It is probably one of the most painstakingly compiled diaries in the history of Indian Muslim literature. There is nothing provisional or arbitrary about its style, production, or presentation. It is a text deliberately created by the author for the people in power.

Ghalib's diary is divided into two main parts: the first part covers the period under the rebel forces; and the second part deals with the British recapture of Delhi. In between these two structuring narratives, Ghalib inserts his personal plea to the British, making the personal a hinge that holds the doors to the public aspects of the work. About the production and publication of the diary, Ahmad Farooqi points out:

> During the revolt Ghalib wrote his diary of the events called *Dastanbuuy* or 'nosegay' in pure Persian with an unwitting admixture of Arabic words and in an oblique style of which he was a master and which the delicate occasion also demanded. (10)

We also know from Ghalib's own account that the diary was supposed to be a well thought out, aptly published, highly deliberate attempt at producing a text. There is nothing arbitrary or diary-like about the production and presentation of the diary. In fact, Ghalib ensured that the diary was published in what he called 'old Persian' without 'the mixture of any Arabic words' (282), although such a mixture would have been common to a multilingual poet's every-day diary writing. Ghalib spends quite a lot of time trying to edit one single Arabic word before the book goes in production. All these aspects of the production of the text clearly dispel any notion in our minds that the diary was not a deliberately written public document.

Considering the circumstances under which the diary was written and published, its importance as a political document is further accentuated. Ghalib publishes the diary in the middle of the post-Rebellion trials of the Indian, mostly Muslim, *shurfaa*. We also know through historical records that Ghalib was afraid of being implicated in the conspiracy of the rebellion.[9] Hence, the diary becomes a legal document, written in the most obscure language, and placed in the hands of the very officials who would decide Ghalib's immediate fate as a wartime nobleman, and also his financial future—his pension.

Equipped with this understanding of the immediate context of the production of the diary, we can now read the text itself. I will begin with Ghalib's account of the fall of the city to the rebels:

> On that infamous day [11 May 1857], the walls and ramparts of the Red Fort shook with such force that the vibrations were felt in the four corners of the city. On that infamous day rebellious soldiers from Meerut, faithless to the salt, entered Delhi thirsty for the blood of the British ... They did not leave their bloody work until they had killed officers and Englishmen, wherever they found them, and had destroyed their homes. (31)

From the very start of Ghalib's narrative, it becomes obvious that the rebellion, to him, is a question of rule of law *versus* anarchy, and a question of loyalty to one's salt. Salt is a very important metaphor to understand. The term in Persian, or Urdu, is *namak-halaal* (loyal), and *namak-haaram* (disloyal), to one's masters or patrons. For Ghalib, the native soldiers who entered the city and disturbed the rule of law had violated the basic covenant of allegiance to one's salt in their act of being disloyal to their employers. This view of the rebels is mediated through two impulses, personal and cultural. Personally, Ghalib must attempt to portray the rebellion as an event involving a specific group, the sepoys, who are, in his view, guilty of disloyalty. This assertion posits the rebellion as specific to a certain class, and not as a general uprising that could claim the support of all social groups of India. Within this specificity, then, Ghalib can insert his own particularity as a helpless loyal subject. Culturally, Ghalib's representation of the rebels also explains the class-specificity of the rebellion. As we will see later, the rebels are portrayed as the common riff-raff, the masses, while Ghalib himself is from the *shurfaa*, hence equally as aggrieved a party as the British. After introducing the rebels, Ghalib then juxtaposes them with an account of those few who were loyal to the British:

> A few poor, reclusive men, who received their bread and salt by the grace of the British, lived scattered ... quite distant from one another. These humble, peaceful people did not know an arrow from an axe; their hands were empty of the sword; and even the sound of the thieves in the dark frightened them ... I was one of these helpless, stricken men. (31)

This passage is quite instructive in highlighting Ghalib's main line of defence against any charges of active involvement and complicity with the rebels. First, Ghalib disrupts the binary of rebels and inhabitants of Delhi

and the British. This brilliantly articulated passage moves the discussion
from a degree of generality—all Muslims of Delhi—to the particularity
of the inhabitants of Delhi, some of whom were not only too weak to
participate in the rebellion, but were also the victims of the anarchy
because of their British loyalties. Their physical location—scattered—also
is important to note for that precludes any possibility of resisting the
rebels and aiding the British, a question that was asked of all the city
inhabitants later tried by the British. Here, Ghalib is being quite prescient,
for this trend to highlight Muslim particularities as opposed to a
generalised view by the British, becomes a cornerstone of the Muslim
negotiation of the British power in the ensuing stages of Muslim national
struggle. Ghalib also displays here the degree of interiority required of a
modern subject, for this particular assertion allows him to tell his own
story, the story of his suffering during the rebellion, which would
eventually help him build a case for British patronage. Thus, even before
it was made public, it is fairly obvious that this document was meant to
prove Ghalib's particular state during the rebellion, and his unquestionable
namakhalali (loyalty) to the British.

The dual temporality of Ghalib's subjectivity—a modern subject
capable of interiority and able to show public human sympathy—is also
one important aspect of the diary. Ghalib laments the loss of the British
during the siege of Delhi by the rebels in the following words:

> Oh, pity those great men, who embodied wisdom, who personified justice—
> those courteous rulers bearing a good name! Oh, pity those fairy-faced, slim-
> bodied women whose faces shone like the moon and whose bodies glittered
> like raw silver! A thousand times pity children, innocent of the world, who
> put roses and tulips to shame....All of these were sucked into the whirlpool of
> death and were drowned in an ocean of blood. (32)

This is Ghalib's humanistic rendition of the plight of the British during
the rebellion. Though we have no reason to doubt his sincerity, Ghalib
becomes the kind of enlightenment subject capable of showing sympathy
for the others. I am taking this aspect of modern subjectivity, with some
modifications, from Dipesh Chakrabarty who explains this concept as
follows:

> The capacity to notice and document suffering (even if it be one's own
> suffering) from the position of a generalised and necessarily disembodied
> observer is what marks the beginning of the modern self. This self has to be
> generalizable in principle; in other words, it should be such that it signifies a

position available for occupation by anybody without proper training....The person who is not an immediate sufferer, but who has the capacity to become a secondary sufferer through sympathy from a generalized picture of suffering, and who documents this suffering in the interest of eventual social intervention—such a person occupies the position of the modern subject. (119)

For Ghalib what happened to the British in the city is not only a breach of the contract of loyalty that the soldiers owed to their British masters, but also a human tragedy. It is this aspect of the native feelings that the British sought in the actions and stances of the natives toward the rebellion. To the British, the only morally apt way of viewing the rebellion was as a universal tragedy, thus it was imperative for Muslims wishing to prove their loyalty that they had either physically aided the British, or that, at least, they had found the acts of the sepoys morally wrong. Ghalib is in the same plight: he must transcend the nativist view of history in order to make a more humanistic claim to British patronage; he must present the rebellion as a tragedy, but as a tragedy from his point of view, as well. Thus, this passage bolsters Ghalib's claim to British sympathy not only through the claim to loyalty, or inability to act rightfully, but also through the sharing of a common sympathy for the victims of the rebellion. Here, Ghalib moves his narrative from the realm of relative politics to the politics of universal sympathy in the language of modernity, a language that his auditors would understand better. This way of writing also becomes a standard for the future articulations of Muslim identity. The Muslim nationalist elite eventually had to master this universal political speech to make their case more convincing to the British. To make any progress, any negotiation of the British power must speak from within the language of power, and that is what Ghalib inaugurates in *Dastanbuuy*.

Another aspect of the diary is its class specificity: Ghalib attempts to differentiate between the class of *shurfaa* and the rebels, which is his partial attempt to further particularise the nature of the rebellion and offer a defence for the *shurfaa* of Delhi, of whom he himself is a part. He, therefore, posits the rebellion as tragedy not only for the British but also for the respectable native inhabitants of India: in Ghalib's view 'throughout the day the rebels looted the city and at night they slept in silken beds,' while 'in the noblemen's houses there is no oil for the lamps' (33). For Ghalib, the rebellion is also a tragedy for the nobles of Delhi whose lives are now under threat from those he calls the 'black-hearted, cowardly robbers' (33). Throughout the diary one finds no sympathy for the cause of the rebels, but there are numerous references as to how the rebellion has destroyed the class hierarchies and destroyed the peace and order of the city, a peace and order that was previously maintained by the just order of the East India Company. In another instructive passage Ghalib explains the upturned socio-political order in the following words:

> Noblemen and great scholars have fallen from power; and the lowly ones, who have never known wealth or honour, now have prestige and unlimited riches. One whose father wandered dust-stained through the streets now proclaims himself ruler of the wind. One whose mother borrowed from neighbour's fire with which to light her kitchen declares himself sovereign of fire. These are the men who hope to rule over fire and wind, and we unhappy ones have no desires left but for moments of respite and a little justice....Tell me, you who believe in law and justice, is there no cause for weeping and breast-beating in the complete breakdown of administration, the looting of God-given wealth, the chaos of the postal system and the failure of news as to the welfare of our relations and friends? (34)

What disturbs Ghalib is something very peculiar to his class-specific view: the lowly order, it seems, has replaced *shurfaa*, the established upper-classes of Delhi. Thus, the revolt has been tragic not only for the British, but also for the local nobility, some of whom, as Ghalib seems to suggest, were British *namak-khwaars* (dependents). This class-specific vision is one reason why Ghalib cannot see any good in the rebellion, but the very nature of the rebellion is reason enough for him to lay claim to a common suffering with the British. Also, by particularizing the rebels as unwanted elements, Ghalib forestalls any attempts at equating all native Muslims as eager participants of the rebellion. This class particularity of the rebellion is in direct opposition to most British accounts of the rebellion. Alexander Duff, for example, offers the following views about the escape of certain rebels through a secret passage during the siege of the fort of Katghur:

> The existence of this passage, though unknown to Sir Hugh's force, must have been well-known to every native in the neighbourhood. And yet not one manifested loyalty enough to disclose the fact to the British chief. Does not a fact like this significantly show on whose side the hearts and wishes of the citizens and peasantry were? And yet we are told that the recent revolt was *nothing* but a *military mutiny*! (208)

It is against this general view of the natives and the rebellion—a view reported regularly through Duff's dispatches—that Ghalib is writing.

Hence, while the first part of *Dastanbuuy* particularises the chaos and the suffering of the elite—including the *shurfaa*, the scholars, and the merchants—at the hands of the 'lowly' rebels, the second part dwells on the plight of the city after the fall of Delhi to the British. It is obvious in this part of the narrative that Ghalib attempts to see the good intentions of the British commanders; he sees them as the just lawgivers, and any atrocities committed by the British soldiers are posited as incidental and anomalous.[10] In this section of the narrative Ghalib also broaches the plight of the post-rebellion Muslims of Delhi, but the narrative is more concerned with human sympathy and does not indict the British for their heavy-handedness. Ghalib describes the recapture of Delhi in the following words:

> On the fourteenth of September...the British who had taken refuge on the outskirts of the ridge, attacked Kashmiri gate with such violence that the rebels were forced into headlong flight... Some of the black-hearted (rebel) army attempted escape, but others, out of pride, were determined to fight and confronted the lion-hearted conquerors... I have told you that when the angry lions entered the town, they killed the helpless and the weak and they burned their houses. It may be that such atrocities always occur after conquests. (40-41)

As the above text demonstrates, the binary is still strictly maintained; it is still the 'dark-hearted' rebels against the British 'angry lions'. And even though there is mention of British atrocities, Ghalib generalises them as a consequence of conquest, instead of holding the British particularly accountable. His approach to the actions of the rebels, as we have seen, is more particularised and critical, but he cannot, because of the public nature of his document and its utilitarian function, indict the British so openly. At another place Ghalib again gives the account of British atrocities with a certain degree of particularity. He writes: 'The manner of killing and looting by the [British] soldiers is not uniform but varies, and whether a soldier shows kindness or unkindness depends on his individual nature' (49).

This account of the British atrocities individualises them instead of representing them as systemic. Hence, all British atrocities are either posited as exceptional or as an integral part of the nature of war.

A moving account of the general plight of the people after the fall of the city to the British is given in the diary. Ever cautious of the choice of words, and without directly blaming the British, Ghalib writes a narrative of the everyday struggles of the people. He thus plays the role of a chronicler of the pain of others. Dipesh Chakrabarty identifies sympathy, according to classical enlightenment thought, as an important attribute of the modern subject. In Ghalib's case, however, we soon move from the outside perspective to the very interiority of the speaking subject: his own struggles, plight, and hopes after the rebellion. Ghalib combines the classical Persian style of address and modern rhetoric to assert his claim as a British dependent, and as a subject worthy of kind British dispensation. This way of self-presentation is inscribed within the very public nature of his diary.

Ghalib tells us that, 'the people have lost all their power to endure' and that, 'these days, we think of ourselves as prisoners and we are, in truth, passing our days like prisoners' (44). Then, after giving us an immediate account of the post-rebellion Delhi, Ghalib moves on to tell his own story: he is now ready to build his case to the British. By now, as the text clearly tells us, he has proved his loyalties to the British, has distanced himself from the rebels, and is writing from the confines of his dilapidated house, as the British are reconsolidating their power over the city. The narrative thus is a political document and should be read as such. Ghalib begins his personal account:

> This is the sixty-second year of my life. For many years I have been straining the dust of this world through a sieve; and for the last fifty years I have been opening the depths of my heart through poetry....My uncle...was the captain of four hundred horsemen and a loyal associate of General Lord Lake Bahadur....I received the pension from the treasury of the Delhi Collectorate until the end of April 1857 when it was closed. Now I am confronted with misfortune and my heart is filled with anxiety. (45-46)

Here again Ghalib starts with the historical precedence of his family's loyalty to the British. He then combines that aspect of loyalty with the material remuneration that he had been receiving until the rebellion occurred. As he has already proved his position about the rebels and the British, he now hopes to make a case for the restoration of his pension. This is the essence of Ghalib's narrative. The entire diary, in fact, is meant to highlight Ghalib's pension case. Ghalib of the diary is a modern subject using his interiority and his doubts and anxieties in changing times to restore what existed before.

Ghalib goes on to narrate the plight of his immediate family who all depend on him, and who are certainly dependent on the restoration of his pension. The claim is made within two interconnected registers of sympathy and loyalty to the new regime. Ghalib then narrates how his pension would have been restored previously. 'Two years ago', he writes, 'I sent a panegyric in praise of the most exalted Queen Victoria, splendid as the stars' (47). He then mentions the entire chain of command of British officials who wrote back to him, proving that, 'had the administration of India not been disturbed during the recent revolt...a royal decree would have been issued from England satisfying all my desires' (49). Hence, while writing in the middle of the rebellion, Ghalib is attempting to efface the very presence of the rebellion itself. He wants his case to be heard as if the rebellion had not happened. After pursuing his particular case further, Ghalib returns to the general plight of the inhabitants of Delhi. His personal request is, therefore, safely couched within the general suffering of the people. Ghalib's first mention of the plight of those who had fled the city is quite neutral and is not specific to their religious affiliation or class identity. He records:

> Most of the citizens had fled the city, but some caught between hope and despair, are still living inside the walls. So far no information has been received about those hiding in lonely places outside of Delhi....The hearts of the helpless inhabitants of the city, and those of the grief-stricken people outside, are filled with sorrow, and they are afraid of mass slaughter. (50)

Ghalib then gives an account of the arrests of the nobles who had supported the rebellion. These nobles include Ahmad Ali Khan, ruler of Farrukhabad, Bahadur Jung Khan, the ruler of Dadri and Bahadurgarh, and Raja Nahar Singh, ruler of Ballabhgarh (56). Only one of these rulers is Hindu, while the other two are Muslims. Thus, in the prosecution of the nobility, without even making an assertion, a pattern of Muslim defeat and prosecution emerges for the reader. Similarly, while writing about the Mughal princes, all of whom were Muslims, Ghalib informs us that 'some were shot...and some were hung by their necks with ropes and, in their twisting, their spirits left them' (57-58). What the narrative invokes then is the beginning of the total destruction of the Muslim nobility and Muslim political power in the post-Rebellion political order.

Ghalib's account of the popular Muslim plight is matter-of-fact, but it does represent the everyday realities of life for the Muslims of Delhi. In this account the differences in the post-rebellion political fortunes of Hindus and Muslims become quite obvious:

> In January 1858, the Hindus were given a proclamation of freedom by which they were allowed to live again in the city....But the houses of dispossessed Muslims had long remained empty and were so covered with vegetation that

the walls seemed to be made of grass—and every blade of grass tells that the house of the Muslim is still empty. (58)

At another place Ghalib gives another brief account of the Muslims living outside the city and then connects his own plight to theirs. He writes: 'In the entire city of Delhi it is impossible to find more than one thousand Muslims; and I am one of these' (60). Ghalib further informs his readers that most of these Muslims want to return to the city and their petitions are awaiting a decision by the local administrator, just as he is 'awaiting a reply to the letter of respect and praise' (61) that he had sent to the new Governor-General, hoping to get his pension restored. Hence, in this account Ghalib links his own plight to that of the other suffering Muslims whose petitions are being held in abeyance: he becomes one of many in his hopes and desires under a new Order.

Ghalib then makes a most interesting claim about his Muslim identity. He writes, 'I am only half Muslim, and quite free from the rigidities of religion' (66). Ghalib considers himself half Muslim because of his drinking habit, for it was his habit 'at night to drink a foreign wine' (66). He then tells us of Mahesh Das, a benefactor, who had been able to provide him his nightly libation. The same Mahesh Das, Ghalib tells us, 'left no stone unturned in his efforts to bring back the Muslims to the city' (66). This fluid movement from the very personal to the public combines a personal assertion that might help Ghalib in his defence, and at the same time moves the reader's attention from something objectionable in Islam to the question of larger good—return of the Muslims—and that too by Ghalib's benefactor who was a Hindu. Such representation problematizes the binary of Ghalib as a sinner, by exalting the same benefactor from the private realm of Ghalib's own life to the very future of Muslims of Delhi.

Towards the end of his narrative Ghalib first conveys his gratitude to all those who had been kind to him during his isolation in Delhi. He then goes on to narrate that he had written this account for his friends, for he wants them to know:

That the city is empty of Muslims—their houses are not lit at night; and during the day their chimneys give forth no smoke. And Ghalib who had thousands of friends in the city…now in his loneliness has none to talk with except his pen; and no companion but his shadow. (67)

This parting message, of course, is for Ghalib's native audience and particularises the plight of the Muslims in a post-rebellion world. The physical exclusion of Muslims from the new dominant regime is the beginning of the struggle of the Muslim elite in their quest for inclusion into the new Order, an inclusion that can only be effected through the language of loyalty. Ghalib ends his narrative with a final request to the Queen, to whom he had already pleaded his pension request. In an interesting concluding passage, Ghalib, after thanking his friends, and narrating the general and particular account of the rebellion, focuses once again on the deeply personal aspect of his pension:

> I have written herein an account of events from May of last year to July 1858. On August first I have laid down my pen. I long for orders from the auspicious sovereign concerning three petitions about which I have written in this book—that is for title, for robe of honour, and for pension. My eyes and my heart look forward to this order from the Empress whose crown is the moon, whose throne is the sky; who is renowned as Jamshid, as splendid as Faridun, as majestic as Kaus, as noble as Sanjar, as exalted as Alexander....If through the generosity of the Queen of the World, I obtain some benefit, I will not have left this life a failure. (69-70)

What are we to learn from Ghalib's narrative about the future nationalistic politics of India? After all, how much of an impact can a diary have on the politics of literary production by Ghalib's co-religionists? The translator of the work informs us that 'of the first edition, five hundred copies of *Dastanbuuy* were sold-out in five months. A second edition was brought out in 1865, and a third in 1871, after Ghalib's death' (21). Part of the reason for the diary's success is, of course, Ghalib's own popularity within the Delhi circles, and the other reason simply is the patronage towards the poet by the elite that they displayed by purchasing a copy of his works.

Dastanbuuy gives us one of the most prominent accounts of the rebellion recorded by the greatest Muslim poet of its time. As the outcome of the rebellion was more of a political tragedy (fall of the Muslim elite and the flight of Muslims from Delhi), Ghalib's narrative, therefore, highlights the very exceptional nature of the Muslim condition after the rebellion. The descriptive narrative of Muslim marginalization becomes emblematic of future Muslim struggles, for the post-rebellion Muslim elite constantly struggled to be included within the hegemonic structures of British power. Eventually, due to relative differences of inclusion in comparison to the Hindus, the idea of Muslim exceptionalism and particularity becomes a core concept in later Muslim demands for a separate electorate and quota system in government jobs. The public nature of Ghalib's diary also points out that almost all post-rebellion negotiations of the British and Muslims can only make sense if read within the realm of politics; culture alone fails to carry the burden of Muslim representation.

NOTES

1. This chapter is reproduced here with the permission of Taylor and Francis Publishers Limited. Previous publication details: "The Indian Rebellion of 1857 and Mirza Ghalib's Narrative of Survival." *Prose Studies* Vol. 31(1) 2009: 40–54.
2. For details about Ghalib's pension petition see P. Hardy, 'Ghalib and the British', *Ghalib: The Poet and his Age*, Ralph Russell, Ed., New Delhi: Oxford University Press, 1997, 54-69.
3. This perception of Ghalib exists in the popular realm only and not in scholarly opinion.
4. By far the best translation in English of Ghalib's selected works is *The Seeing Eye* by Ralph Russell.
5. For a good explanation of *Sharif* culture See David Lelyveld, *Aligarh's First Generation: Muslim Solidarity in British India*, 35-92.
6. The page numbers for Ambedkar's work are from a privately bound copy and may not correspond to a published copy. B.R. Ambedkar, *Pakistan or the Partition of India*, 1945. The text is also available on line: http://www.Columbia.edu/itc/mealac/Pritchett/ 00ambedkar, 17 July 2009.
7. All citations from Ghalib's Urdu letters are from Volume 1 and are in my translation.
8. For details on this particular habit of Ghalib see Muhammad Sadiq, *A History of Urdu Literature*, 164-209.
9. According to Khwaja Ahmad Farooqi, Ghalib 'attended the Mughal court frequently during the revolt of 1857, fully shared the jubilation of Indians on the fall of Agra' (19).
10. This has been one of the most important imperial strategies and even finds its expression in our own times in the rhetoric of the United States government about the Abu Ghraib torture case in Iraq. The US policy makers insisted that it should be seen as acts of individual transgression and not as systemic, for the latter is an indefensible moral position as it diminishes the moral superiority needed to justify the imperial project.

2

Post-Rebellion India and the Rise of Muslim Exceptionalism

The political landscape altered drastically in post-rebellion India. While for the British it started the final phase of the consolidation and legitimation of the raj, for the Muslims of India the beginning of the raj also initiated the politics of the popular, in which the Muslim imaginary was constantly haunted by their loss of power, their immediate condition after the rebellion, and their anxieties about a political future. Overall, a general mythology of Muslim troubles and backwardness took hold and launched the multifaceted Muslim campaign for creating a particularly Muslim space within the British system.

As stated earlier, the Muslim perception of politics was transformed after the rebellion, but so was the British view of Indian politics. The so-called Muslim *question* became critical to the British, and it became imperative for them to work towards creating a hegemonic relationship with India's Muslims. It was this need of the British to create their hegemony and the Muslim attempts to be included within the British hegemonic structure that eventually brought about the idea of Muslim nationhood. The practice of divide-and-rule in India has been broached by many a scholar, but what really needs to be studied is that the whole edifice of British power in India depended upon creating a hegemonic relationship with the Muslims of India. This chapter explores some seminal British and Muslim texts to tease out the genesis of the idea of Muslim exceptionalism and the centrality of the Muslim question to the post-rebellion British policies.

Before I attempt a textual analysis of my chosen texts, I find it apt to first provide a brief discussion of Paul Brass's *Language, Religion and Politics in North India*, for this chapter, in a way, challenges Brass's main assertion about the rise of Muslim national consciousness. In a chapter entitled 'Muslim Separatism in the United Provinces' Paul Brass questions the established historical assumptions about the nature of Hindu–Muslim differences. Brass sums up these flawed historical assumptions as the idea of 'the backwardness of the Muslims compared to the Hindus', the failure of the Muslim elite to 'compete with Hindus for English education and government jobs', and finally, a belief that the Hindus 'took advantage of the new opportunities and moved ahead of the Muslims' (120). In response to these normative assumptions in Indian historiography, Brass suggests:

> This entire argument and its assumptions do not apply to the United Provinces and...the objective situation in the late-nineteenth and early-twentieth centuries in the United Provinces was in most respects exactly the opposite of that described above. (121)

Thus, the main crux of Brass's argument is that the traditionally held views about the relative backwardness of Muslims as compared to Hindus did not really exist in the United Provinces; but rather this perception develops as a mobilizing strategy against the actual existing conditions that were not so terrible for the Muslims of United Provinces. Brass also moves on to trace the real cause of such commonly held views by the Muslim elite and the populace. Thus, in Brass's view, 'a myth which originated in yearnings by an upper class for the maintenance of aristocratic privilege...when attached to the theory of Muslim backwardness, became later, a means of uniting elites and mass in the Muslim community by exploiting fears of Hindu dominance' (140). Brass provides one British text as the core source of this myth-making process: W.W. Hunter's *The Indian Musalmans*, published in 1871. In Brass's view, then, the so-called communal disparity did not exist in the United Provinces, and the mobilisation of the myth of Muslim backwardness owed its birth to the published text of a British civil servant. Brass opines as follows about Hunter's text and its attendant impact on the Muslim politics:

> Hunter's arguments, generalised for the whole India, soon became integrated, with embellishments, into the minds of Muslim elites, who used them to appeal to the British policy-makers and later to the Muslim masses to separate the Muslim from Hindu interests. (141)

Thus, interestingly, we are told that not only did the Muslims of United Provinces have no factual basis for any sort of particular communal grievances, but that even the myth of such grievance percolated down to the Muslims through a work produced by a British official. The native, it seems, is not even capable of imagining and visualizing his own condition under a new regime. Of course, Brass's misplaced assertion has already been complicated in the first chapter, for Ghalib's account of the rebellion is already an incipient narrative of Muslim particularity, but this chapter, I hope, will convincingly refute Brass's version of the downward filtration theory. In the ensuing pages I juxtapose Hunter's work with that of Sayyid Ahmad Khan's to suggest, among other things, that the idea of Muslim particularity was shaped much earlier than Hunter's putative work about the Muslims was published.

SAYYID AHMAD KHAN: *THE CAUSES OF THE INDIAN REVOLT*

Published in Urdu in 1859, *Asbab-e-Baghawat-e-Hind* was the first detailed Muslim treatment of the specific causes of the 1857 Rebellion, especially due to its focus on the particularities of the Muslim involvement in the rebellion. The author, a survivor of the rebellion and a British Indian Civil Servant, lays down through this particular document the foundations of what later, at least in Muslim elite historiography, becomes the idea of Muslim exceptionalism. Sayyid Ahmad's account also dispels the overarching Cambridge thesis that it was the European stimulus that launched the liberal notion of citizenship and eventually nationalistic politics. I will, henceforth, discuss the process of production of this particular text as well as its eventual appropriation by the Muslim freedom movement. It is this particular document that became instrumental in making the Muslim question central to the British administration of India from the point of view of the Muslim natives of India.

The writing and publication of *The Causes of the Indian Revolt* was not without its attendant dangers. Sir Sayyid's biographer, Altaf Hussain Hali informs us that post-rebellion India 'was an exceedingly dangerous period. There was no freedom whatsoever to voice ones opinions' (91). Hali also declares that conditions were exceedingly harsh for the Muslims. 'To incriminate a Muslim,' he writes, 'there was no need for any proof' (91). It was under such perilous circumstances that Sayyid Ahmad Khan wrote this particular work: a political narrative of courage aimed at affecting and altering the British view of their Muslim subjects. This narrative, in its very materiality and means of production, also defies the European stimulus thesis and places the agency of creating a Muslim response within the native structures of the public imperative: the need for the elite to speak for, and work in the name of the people to legitimate their own place within the British political order. The attempt was not without its dangers for the work was produced at the height of British dominance over India where a hegemonic relationship related to the bourgeois liberal discourse of rights had not been established, for the country was 'under martial law' (Hali 91). Hali also informs us that 'when the work was finished, without waiting for an English translation, Sir Sayyid sent the Urdu version to be printed' (93). When the printed copies were received Sayyid's friends beseeched him 'not to send the pamphlet to the parliament or the Government of India' (93). Yet another of his friends 'begged him to burn the books rather than put his life in danger' (93). Sayyid replied that:

> He was bringing these matters to the attention of the British for the *good of his own people*, of his country and of the government itself. He [also] said that if he came to any harm while doing something that would greatly benefit the rulers and the subjects of India alike, he would gratefully suffer whatever befell him. (Emphasis added, 93)

There are two aspects of Sayyid's lived experience that lend him the courage to converse with a very dictatorial regime of his time: he can make his claims under the rubric of loyalty, which he had already proven during the rebellion,[1] and by employing what Ranjit Guha calls the idiom of obedience ('Dominance Without' 252). The work was not distributed in India, but 'almost all the 500 copies [were] sent to England' (Hali 94). Hence, this particular work was written primarily for a British audience, where, Hali points out, it was 'discussed by Parliament' (96). The editors of this particular edition of the pamphlet inform us that when it was finally discussed in the British Parliament, the Foreign Secretary, Cecil Baton, 'made a strong speech against it and said that this person had written a very seditionary essay, and that he should be interrogated and punished accordingly' (Khan 8). This suggests that *The Causes of the Indian Revolt*, though it entered native Muslim politics at a later stage, did launch a series of parliamentary discussions in England, and was important in highlighting the particularity of the Muslim situation, and certainly made the question of Muslim grievances central to the British parliamentary discussion of India.

The Causes of the Indian Revolt is divided into two major parts: the first refutes all the reasons forwarded about the rebellion by the British press and men of letters; while the second explains the causes from a native, often Muslim, point of view. Sayyid Ahmad Khan first gives the main cause of the rebellion and then goes on to explain its attendant ramifications under five separate registers. To him, rebellion is a terminal manifestation of a long process of native grievances against their British administration. In his words, 'a vast store of explosive material had been collected. It wanted but the application of a match to light it; and that match was applied by the Mutinous army' (53). Hence, from the very start, Sir Sayyid aims to dispel the notion of a spontaneous event fuelled by religious fanaticism and hatred into a process which ensures that, if the contours of this process are outlined, then a long rehabilitative phase could replace the retributive and summary justice that followed the rebellion. Sir Sayyid goes on to articulate the main reason for the rebellion:

> I believe this Rebellion owes its origin to one great cause to which all others are but secondary branches, so to speak, of the parent stem... Most men, I believe, agree in thinking that it is highly conducive to the welfare and prosperity of Government...that people should have voice in its Councils. It is from the *voice of the people* only that governments can learn whether its projects are likely to be well received...There is no reason why the natives of this country should be excluded from the Legislative Council and, hence, it is that you come upon the one great root of all this evil...From causes connected with this matter sprang all the evil that has lately happened. (61-3).

Sir Sayyid does not argue about the native lack of representation from within the norms of a liberal bourgeois vision of a civic state, but rather from a different utilitarian paradigm. The purpose of the native representatives is to act as native informants who can 'teach' the government a better way of reaching the native populations, for the government 'has not succeeded in acquainting itself with the daily habits, the modes of thought and of life, the likes and dislikes, and the prejudices of the people' (63). Here lies the crux of Sir Sayyid's whole argument: the British need to create a native collaborator class upon which the whole edifice of the raj can stand; in other words, a move from the mercantile dominant policies of the East India Company to the future hegemony of the raj. At this stage, it must be noted that Sir Sayyid cannot argue from within the bourgeois liberal ideal of equal representation; he must instead argue from the perspective of the utility of native participation to the raj, and he must also argue on the plane of obedience under the general rubric of loyalty. Thus, as a text with a specific focus on the plight of Muslims, Sir Sayyid's pamphlet ensures the creation of a space for Muslims within the British administration of India, and his timely intervention precedes any British works about the subject.

Sir Sayyid then goes on to explain the concomitant consequences of the lack of native representation under five different areas. All these five arguments highlight the importance of native informants, for if there had been such a class, such misunderstanding of the British administration would have not arisen in the first place. Consequently, through this one document Sir Sayyid writes, the native informant, who had previously been foreclosed, into the very fibre of the British administration of India. Sir Sayyid lists the five concomitant causes of the native lack of representation as follows:

1. Ignorance on the part of the people: by which I mean mis-apprehension of the intentions of the government.
2. The passing of such laws and regulations and forms of procedure as jarred with the established customs and practice of Hindustan, and the introduction of such were in themselves objectionable.
3. Ignorance on the part of the government of the condition of the people—; of their modes of thought and of life; and of the grievances through which their hearts were becoming estranged.
4. The neglect on the part of our rulers of such points as were essential to the good governance of Hindustan.
5. The bad management and disaffection of the army. (65-6)

Together these five points are a total reversal of the British view of the rebellion: except for the first point that places some blame on the natives for misreading government policies, all the other points shift the blame onto the East India Company and the local administrators of India. And since the argument is forwarded by a faithful Muslim under the rubric of loyalty and general welfare of the raj, the document then becomes a native manuscript for better governance of India, an instruction manual from the governed to those who govern them. This document, therefore, creates a space for the native to speak from, and, because of its Muslim specificity, forces the British discourse of India from the practice of sheer dominance towards the realisation of a workable hegemony. Considered together, all these points seriously highlight the need for a comprador class: a class of natives who can translate the local culture for the British administrators. Note that Sayyid is not asking for parity with the English, nor is he asking for equal rights: he cannot ask for that at this stage of the colonial encounter. Instead, he is attempting to create a space for the native elite within the new order, and that space can only be created from the point of view of the administrative efficiency of the raj itself and not on the basis of inalienable rights for all individuals within the bourgeois liberal project.

In explaining his first point, Sir Saiyyid clearly states that his main concern is not the actual policies of the British, but rather, their interpretation by the natives. The whole problem then is the problem of cultural translation. He begins:

> I would here say that I do not wish it to be understood that the views of the Government were in reality such as have been imputed to them. I only wish to say that they were misconstrued by the people, and that this misconstruction hurried on the Rebellion. *Had there been a native of Hindustan in the Legislative Council, the people would never have fallen into such errors.* (Emphasis added, 66)

This particular argument begins with the general religious anxieties of both Muslims and Hindus, for they believed that, 'the Government intended to force the Christian Religion and foreign customs upon Hindu and Mussalman alike' (66). Eventually, however, the argument becomes specific to the Muslim anxieties: Sir Sayyid suggests that the people feared that having established its dominance in the region and 'as the power of the Government increased…it would turn its attention inwards, and carry out a more systematic interference with their creed and religious observances' (67). The most important reason for such a popular perception, Sir Sayyid suggests, is because the people 'believed that the Government appointed Missionaries and maintained them at its own cost' (67). Sir Sayyid also touches upon the differences in religious practices of the natives and the missionaries. He suggests that traditionally, the preaching of religion was a private affair and people did it in the mosque or at their own house: missionaries had violated this contract by preaching publicly (68). Similarly, Sir Sayyid links the same anxieties to the missionary and the village schools, which people saw as tools for native conversion to Christianity. What Sir Sayyid seems to assert here is that even if these steps were taken to facilitate the government or to simply educate the people, the lack of native cultural translators allowed the rumours to be concretised as popularly held beliefs, adding yet one more reason for the rebellion. He then gives an account of a particular missionary document and its misreading by the native public. The letter by a missionary, Mr Edmond, in Sir Sayyid's views expressed the following:

It was to the effect that all Hindustan was now under one rule; that the telegraph had so connected all parts of the country that they were as one...the time had clearly come when there should be but one faith. (72).

As this private document was circulated through public means, and mailed to public servants particularly, it suggested that proselytizing had now become public policy of the government. And even though the Lieutenant Governor of Bengal issued a public denouncement of this particular missionary circular 'men still thought that the Government had given up its projects only for a while' (73). Having laid down a broad and specific argument for native anxieties about a possible Christianisation of the natives, Sir Sayyid then particularises the Muslim response, a sort of nascent Muslim exceptionalism. Based on highly essentialised ideas of the religious identities of Hindus and Muslims, this is where the argument of the text becomes Muslim-specific. Sir Sayyid writes:

> All these causes rendered the Mahommadans [*sic*] more uneasy than the Hindus. The reason for this, I take to be that the Hindu faith consists rather in the practice of long established rites and forms, than the study of doctrine. The Hindus recognise no canons and laws, or appeals to the heart and conscience...hence it is that they are exceedingly indifferent about speculative doctrine. They insist upon nothing, excepting the strict observance of their old rites, and of their modes of eating and drinking. It does not annoy or grieve them, to see such rites and observances, as they consider necessary, disregarded by other men. Mahommadans, on the contrary, looking upon the tenets of their creed as necessary to Salvation...are thoroughly well-grounded in them. They regard their religious precepts as the ordinances of God. Hence, it was that the Mahommadans were more uneasy than the Hindus, and that, as might have been expected, they formed the majority of the rebels. (73)

I would like to dwell a little upon the translation of this passage: it fails to capture the true import of Sir Sayyid's argument, and if read in such a way it can simplify his argument in terms of the differences of a naturalised, unconscious practice of rites (Hinduism); and that of a faith based on canonical law and choice (Islam). The difference between the two main religions involved here can be more aptly, and closely, translated as follows:[2]

> The Muslims were more annoyed with these developments than Hindus. This is because the Hindus perform their religious rites according to custom and not as commands of their religion. They are not aware of the precepts, articles of faith, upon which their salvation may depend, and it is not in their common

usage. Hence, in the practice of their religion, other than normal customs of eating and drinking, they are not so rigid and prejudiced. For them as long as they can hold their own faith in their hearts, it does not trouble them if someone speaks against it. (47)

It becomes obvious through this brief translation that Sir Sayyid is not claiming that Hinduism is static and ossified in custom as compared to a more dynamic Islam. Rather, he finds Hinduism secure in its practices and, therefore, not troubled by contamination from outside. Islam, on the other hand, is based on textual interpretation as well as an idea of a hereafter, thus more insecure and sensitive to any outside threat. This argument also suggests that while Hindus could still exist in their faith despite Christian propaganda, the Muslims saw the same as a threat due to this perpetual sense of crisis. This aspect of Muslim anxiety about their religious way of life later becomes one of the main tropes in the Muslim freedom movement. What Sir Sayyid inaugurates is the specific idea of the Islamic negotiation of the changing political realities. Of course, the emphasis here is not to prove that his argument is right or wrong, but how this argument plays a role in articulating Muslim exceptionalism within his text and later. By this claim, however, he is able to establish that Muslim anxieties about Christian influences are different because of a different world-view and hence need a special dispensation. This line of argument also particularises the Muslim situation and ensures that if his text is to be taken seriously, then the British must create a specific space for the Muslim native elite to act as cultural informants and interpreters, for only they can truly translate the governmental policy to their Muslim constituencies and vice versa.

In explaining the second cause of native discontent, Sir Sayyid moves from questions of native perception of the acts attributed to the government to the actual laws and acts passed by the government. Hence, this and the other three points seek to prove the wrongs of the government, and of course, the remedy for the wrongs has already been provided through the agency of native representation. Despite its attempt to list the grievances of both Hindus and Muslims, Sir Sayyid continues to particularise Muslim grievances, thereby creating a space for Muslims within the raj.

In explaining the second concomitant cause of the rebellion, Sir Sayyid emphasises the role played by the British administration. He begins: 'The Legislative Council is not free from the charge of having meddled with religious matters' (74). Here the need for native informants is further accentuated, for the question is not only how to preclude the wrong interpretation of the actions of the British, but also, how to ensure that no such laws are henceforth passed that could increase religious tensions and undermine British authority in India. Sir Sayyid then goes on to give specific examples of the acts and laws promulgated by the legislative council; and the grievances caused by them. Here again, the general subject is the Indian native, but the Muslims clearly receive specific attention; hence, the entire argument then articulates itself about the question of laws; and the place of Muslims as subjects of such laws.

Sir Sayyid begins the discussion of his second cause with a reference to the Indian Act XXI of 1850.[3] He finds this particular act of legislation especially detrimental to Muslim interests, both in material and spiritual terms. He asserts that, 'this Act was thought to have been passed with the view of cozening men into Christianity' (74). Also, in terms of its material advantages, it was the Muslims rather than the Hindus, who seemed to have been targeted. As the Act dealt with the rules of inheritance based on conversion, it did not affect Hindus for, according to Sir Sayyid, 'the Hindu faith … allows no converts' (74). As no Muslim converts could benefit from this Act, it was deemed that it was not only meant 'to interfere with people's religion, but to hold out a strong inducement to conversion' (74). The discussion of this particular law not only, therefore, foregrounds the Muslim view of the legislative process, but it also points out that for the Muslims, such laws were not merely laws, but were also seen as the British government's way of isolating the Muslims, which accentuated the Muslim distrust of the government. Note that Sir Sayyid is not citing the concerns of the elite;, but rather of the people: his indictment of the legislative policies must invoke the people, for the purpose is to force the British to include native informants in the legislative councils who would be able to instruct the government about the likely popular interpretation of laws to forestall the possibilities of another rebellion.

The discussion of Act XV of 1856[4] explains Hindu anxieties about family law and the rights of widows. Here, Sir Sayyid's approach is more cosmopolitan and less restricted to Muslim concerns, but after concluding his discussion of this particular act he moves on to suggest how sometimes decisions of the courts involving people of the same religion tend to aggravate the problem and generate more distrust of the government. This particular point suggests that any attempt to write religion out of the courts would cause trouble, but that if the contestants are both of the same faith, then it might favour the government if 'the decrees issued by the courts should be in accordance with the religious practice of the parties' (75). What he is suggesting then is that one universal secular legal code cannot meet the requirements of the whole of India, and that wherever possible the government should accommodate the religious legal code if the litigants share the same religion.

The rest of the discussion is about the material outcome of the land and revenue acts, which, in Sir Sayyid's view, are the main area of problem of the British legal system. It is here that a narrative of the local elite develops in Sir Sayyid's argument. The debate moves on from the realm of the popular to the realm of the elite. Here, Sir Sayyid also invokes the historical precedent of landowning and taxation; he even compares the British land revenue laws with the positive laws that existed before, which, of course, make it imperative to engage the native elite in promulgating land revenue laws. I will only briefly cite his comparison of the land taxes to qualify my point:

> Akbar [the Great] divided the land into classes, and changed the payments in kind into money payments. The first class...by the name of 'Pulich' was cultivated yearly, and the produce of this he divided with the cultivators according to their respective shares. The second class, was called 'Paroti' and was not kept in constant cultivation.... The produce of this class of land he shared with the cultivators in such years as it was cultivated. The third class...called 'Chachar' remained uncultivated for 3 to 4 years, and required the expenditure of money in order to make it fertile. In the first year of cultivation, Akbar took two-fifths of the produce...increasing his demand yearly, till in the fifth year, he received his full share. The fourth class which was called 'Bunjar', and required to lie fallow for more than five years, was treated on still more lenient terms.[5] (79)

The above passage displays the intricate degree of detail involved in the Mughal land revenue system: a system that taxed qualitatively and not quantitatively. The blanket taxation of the land by the British, Sir Sayyid suggests, not only reduced productivity but also put the landholding classes in financial ruin who now 'look back with regret on the dynasties of former days' (80). Note the grievances of landholders here are not posited in terms of loss of power or distrust of the government but on the level of the efficiency of the taxation system. Driven to their ruin by a less accurate system of land taxation, one could argue, the landowners could become willing participants in a rebellion that might replace the present system with a former one that they considered just. This summary explanation of the British laws also strikes the British ideology at its very core, for what could be worse than to realise that, despite their advanced administrative techniques, the British did not fare quite as well as compared to the former rulers of India.

The third cause of the rebellion, according to Sir Sayyid, is the ignorance on the part of the British administration about 'the state of the country and their subjects' (83). He explains the reasons for this ignorance:

> There was no real communication between the Governors and the governed, no living together or near one another, as has always been the custom of the Mahommadans in countries they subjected to their rule.... It is however not easy to see how this can be done by the English as they almost look forward to retirement in their native land and seldom settle for good amongst the natives of India. (83)

This is a searing indictment of the mercantile and non-assimilationist approach of the British administration. What it implies is that, for the government to have a deeper knowledge of its subjects, it cannot just keep the posture of an overseas empire; it must portray an intent to stay. Furthermore, its officials must have, like the earlier invaders of India, a stake in the day-to-day affairs of the country. Hegemony, it seems, cannot just be enforced by a system that tends to stay outside the sphere of the governed; the British as participants within Indian affairs must create it. Had this government been in touch with its people and considered them to be a part of the whole system, Sir Sayyid contends, it would have had more access to the feelings and grievances of the people. In a nutshell, it is an expectation of national and not colonial government, for any civil government must, in order to seek consent, make an attempt at understanding the problems of the people and then represent itself as a benevolent government. Sir Sayyid explains:

> There is nothing wonderful in the fact that the natives were poor and in distress. A native's best profession is [government] service. Now, although, everyone felt the difficulty of getting into the service, this difficulty pressed most heavily on the Mahommadans....The Mahommadans [as opposed to Hindus] are not the aborigines of this country. They came in the train of former conquerors and gradually domesticated themselves in India. They were, therefore, all dependent on service, and on account of this increased difficulty in obtaining the same, they, far more than the Hindoos, were put to much inconvenience and misery. (85)

This is how Sir Sayyid particularises the Muslim state of being under the British and bolsters the claim of Muslim exceptionalism. Since the Muslims have a different history and since they have always depended upon government service for their sustenance, the British must also continue this policy of providing jobs for the Muslims or else the rebellion may repeat itself. Although Sir Sayyid does not cite any figures or statistics, he does create a logical narrative of Muslim material losses under the British, and to some extent, this is enough to create a future narrative of Muslim exceptionalism. This claim also makes it important for the British to come up with a strategy of transforming possible future mutinous citizens into willing and dependent subjects of the raj, hence, making the Muslim issue central to the functioning of the raj.

Sir Sayyid's fourth argument is clearly focused on the concept of governmentality itself: 'Neglect in matters which should have received consideration from government' (88). The narrative, therefore, moves from the realm of native grievances to the question of British governmental failure. It is important to note here that Sir Sayyid puts forth his argument in the language of love and care—a paternalistic function—but it could also easily be read as an argument of rights; which informs us that the discourse of rights was not just initiated by the downward filtration of European ideas, but that the native culture had its own vocabulary to invoke the rights of the citizens:

> I cannot here state at length what the benefits of friendship, intercourse and sympathy are, but I maintain that the maintenance of friendly relations between the governors and governed is far more necessary than between individuals. Private friendships only affect a few, friendship and good feeling between Government and its subjects affects a whole nation. (88)

Before attempting to unpack the claims forwarded in this passage I must point out an important discrepancy in the translation: The term *muhabbat* is translated as friendship here. In order to reconstruct what Sir Sayyid is actually implying here, it is necessary to retranslate this passage and then read both translations comparatively:. The same passage can also be translated as follows:

> It is important to stress here that the government's love is more important than [private] mutual love and friendship towards one's neighbours. While friendship may involve love of one for another; governmental love must be for all its subjects. *The lover and the beloved are two people who unite as one when*

their hearts are united. Similarly, the government must also develop such a closeness to its people that they become one body. (Emphasis added, 64)

When the two translations are compared, one learns that Sir Sayyid is arguing not just for imperial benevolence, but also for a relationship based on love, the kind of love that unites the governors and the governed as one. The relationship, therefore, must be based on equality and compassion, the very concept of nationhood that, we are told, came to India from post-enlightenment Europe. Sir Sayyid, of course, is claiming this relationship through the Islamic concept of *akhuwwat* (love). Hence, his demand is for a government that works through hegemony and not through dominance alone. Note also that this way of government is desired for all people, since he uses the term *riaya* (people), and not just for the Indian elite. Of course, this love and oneness are impossible to achieve if there is disparity between the lover and the beloved.

To highlight his claim, Sir Sayyid once again invokes the past governments of India. He states: 'A feeling of cordiality was first established in the reign of the Mughal Emperor Akbar I and continued till the reign of Shah Jehan' (91). Thus, what he expects of the British is not just based on an abstract idea of people–government relations but something that already existed in Indian history. This history, it seems, cannot just be obliterated, and it might serve as a beacon for the new conquerors of India in the process of developing their governmental procedures. Thus, from Sir Sayyid's point of view, the need for creating such hegemony demands that the elite informant must be rewritten into history and made an important instrument of the new hegemonic project.

Based on this historical comparison, Sir Sayyid goes on to forward a politics of honour and entitlement, a better way of harnessing the local elite for the imperial project. Sir Sayyid links this with the dissatisfaction of Muslims for their 'exclusion' from 'high appointments' (94). Here, Sir Sayyid also comments upon the superior services examination that all natives are required to pass for them to qualify for government jobs. He asks here, 'are the best amongst the British statesmen those who have passed the high examination? Are high diplomatic posts not often given to them on account of their birth and practical common sense and sometimes without the latter qualification?' (95). Thus, through this comparison, Sir Sayyid is demanding that the same standards be applied to both native and British nobility. Exceptions must be made, based on birth and lineage, and not just academic merit. If such a measure is adopted, it would automatically outflank the *de facto* exclusion of Muslims from the civil services. He probably made this assertion, since, at that time, there were not many academically qualified Muslim candidates for the higher echelon jobs in the British administration of India.

The fifth and final cause of the rebellion deals with the administrative structuring of the military, i.e. the causes for the insubordination of the Indian army. In fact, this is the one cause that shook the confidence of the British in India, for without absolute loyalty from the Royal Indian army—predominantly composed of native soldiers—the very existence of the raj was at stake. Surprisingly, here Sir Sayyid suggests that it was the British practice of combining two 'antagonistic races in the same regiment' that eliminated race rivalries and united them against their British officers. It seems that in organizing the army, the British themselves had failed to follow the general policy of divide and rule. It might have been caused by the strong indoctrinating project of the army, but for Sir Sayyid this became a root cause of the mutiny. Sir Sayyid suggests, 'the difference which exists between Hindoos and Mahammodans had been mostly smoothed away' (100). Thus, the British idea of creating a certain unity within the army in itself became a motivating factor behind a joint rebellion. Sir Sayyid suggests that if 'separate regiments of Hindoos and Mahamoddans had been raised...the Mahamoddan regiments would not have refused to receive the new cartridges' (101). The Muslim sepoys had revolted under the same pretext as their Hindu counterparts, because they shared a common interest, but if their concerns had been isolated from their Hindu counterparts then they would not have followed suit. This also suggests that if the British were to rely on Muslim soldiers in future, their degree of loyalty would be greater than the Hindus, especially since the Muslims are a people who rely on government service for their sustenance. On the whole, then, this argument also aims at creating a sense of exceptionalism for the Muslim masses as well as the elite. Sir Sayyid concludes his argument by attempting to explain the reasons why the Punjab had not participated in the rebellion, for the 'poverty which was so rife in Hindustan had not yet had time to become rife in the Punjab' (104).

On the whole, this particular document is the first native Muslim intervention into the political narrative of the raj. Considering that the document was extensively discussed in the British parliament, and that Sir Sayyid continued to produce other works that highlighted the state of Muslims in India, it is not hard to suggest that Sir Sayyid inaugurates a specific narrative of the general state of Muslims under the British. The document is also instrumental in creating a tradition of political narrative that dwells on the specificity of the Muslim condition under the British; and eventually serves as a model for Muslim claims of particularity within the collectivity governed by the British in India.

I am not attempting to ascertain the veracity of Sir Sayyid's claim, for that would assume the presence of an objective history void of ideology and circumstantial biases. Rather, I am trying to trace how a Muslim intellectual posits a sense of history and represents his people, and how his writing then becomes an archive and a monument, both in the British and in the Muslim political imaginary. It is important to note that all these reasons for the rebellion catch the raj at its most vulnerable position in its Indian politics: a time when the fear that the natives could rise and massacre their own masters and army officers had suddenly become a reality. Written as a period piece, the text transcends its time constraints and eventually becomes the basis of Muslim exceptionalism.

Sayyid Ahmad Khan's political and literary career does not end here; rather, this text launches his career as a British loyalist and a Muslim reformer. What he inaugurates is the two-sidedness of the native experience: the Hindu majority and the Muslim minority. From this point onward, the single most important aspect of Muslim elite politics is to define a Muslim space within the new collectivity. Consequently, except for a few religious and nationalist groups, the Muslims choose to imagine Hindus, rather than the raj, as the 'other': within that context they seek special privileges, including eventually a separate nation-state, in return for their services rendered to the raj. Sir Sayyid, of course, continues with his career as a reformer, and his discursive treatment of Muslim particularity eventually becomes the basis for the idea of a separate Muslim nation.

Naturally, quite a few British texts were written about the rebellion of 1857 and the Muslim role in it. The most important of these texts is W.W. Hunter's *Indian Musalmans*, a text that Paul Brass, as discussed above, erroneously considers a seminal text for launching the myth of Muslim backwardness. I will now turn to this particular text to highlight the importance of the Muslim question for the British administration after the rebellion from the British point-of-view.

W.W. HUNTER'S *INDIAN MUSALMANS* AND MUSLIM RESPONSES

Published in 1871, *The Indian Musalmans* is a political document focusing on one particular aspect of Indian–Muslim politics: the so-called Wahabi Movement in the North-West Frontier Province (NWFP) of India. However, due to the fluid signification of the Muslims in the text, it cannot be read only in its particularity. The text extrapolates from its particularities to suggest a certain generalised argument about the Muslims of India. Hunter's polemic can be considered the central text of the British negotiation of the Muslim question, while also claiming to be one of the first British political documents that invite numerous Muslim responses. I will first juxtapose two parallel texts of the late nineteenth century: W.W. Hunter's *The Indian Musalmans* and Ja'fer Thanesari's *Kala Pani*,[6] English and Urdu texts, respectively, and then briefly analyse Sayyid Ahmad Khan's response to Hunter's book. This brief discussion will highlight the importance of post-rebellion Muslim politics and the centrality of the Muslim question to the post-rebellion British administration of India. Hunter begins his book with a fair degree of particularity while dedicating it to Brian Houghton Hodgson:

> In these pages I have tried to bring out in clear relief the past history and present requirements of a persistently belligerent class—of a class whom successive governments have declared to be a source of permanent danger to the Indian Empire. (i)

So far, the reader does not really know the nature of this particular class, but the title suggests that this particular class may be construed as Muslims in general, and also as a specific Muslim group. The term 'class' is certainly not used in the Marxist sense of the word; rather, it refers to a specific group within the people who pose a great threat to British India. The publishers also tell us that this particular polemic was written in response to a certain question posed by Lord Mayo: 'Are the Indian Muslims bound by their religion to rebel against the Queen?' This question in itself, to which the book is a reply, highlights the degree of Muslim particularity to British interest and the centrality of the Muslim question to the British administration of India. Hunter's work is written with a specific backdrop of the ostensible Wahabi Trials,[7] and with a broader spectrum of the Muslim–British relationship, hence the Viceroy's question. In four chapters, Hunter provides his readers with the historical details of the rebel camp located in the NWFP, then goes on to prove how deep and widespread this conspiracy is, and finally, details the steps the British need to take in order to quell the rebellion in particular, and how best to deal with the Muslim question in general. Hunter's work, therefore, extrapolates from a particularity in order to give a generalised account of the policies necessitated by such a situation. On the whole, the work makes the Muslim question central to the creation of British hegemony over India. [His recommendations suggest that dominance alone would not solve the problem].

Hunter begins his polemic with a particular emphasis on the rebels in the NWFP. He asserts: 'For years a Rebel Colony has threatened our Frontier' (1). He then suggests that this colony is not local, but rather supported by 'an unbroken chain of treason depots' (1). Thus, from the very outset this constant rebel colony, whose members often invade British territories, is endowed with a degree of particularity. Its support base, however, can be generalised as the entire northern regions of India. Hunter's narrative sets up its own logic: a particular Muslim resistance group should be seen in its widest generalisation in terms of its support infrastructure. Hunter's implied thesis is: if nothing is done, this localised rebellion could become a much larger cause involving, probably, the entire Muslim population of Northern India. He also asserts in his book that this rebel camp is not an exception for, 'the *whole* Muhammadan community has been openly deliberating on their obligation to rebel (emphasis added 1). By focusing on one particular Muslim group, Hunter's book lays bare its intention to answer the question regarding the Muslim obligation to revolt. He expresses his main concern in the following words:

> The Musalmans of India are, and have been for many years, a source of chronic danger to the British Power in India. For some reason or other they have held aloof from our system, and the changes in which the more flexible Hindus have cheerfully acquiesced are regarded by them as deep personal wrongs. (3)

This passage invokes two colonial stereotypes: Ariel and Caliban.[8] Hunter makes two very interesting assertions about Hindus and Muslims as the two major political groups of India. In his view, the Hindus have been arielised, while the Muslims were still calibanistic in their acceptance of colonial power. What Hunter is trying to answer is not just Lord Mayo's question, but also the larger question of Muslim assimilation into the British system. In order to accomplish his task, then, Hunter must sacrifice the particularity of the historical case under study, and provide the possibilities of its generalisation to a larger Muslim population. Hunter, therefore, must imagine a Muslim population generally hostile to the British and then suggest some measures to improve the situation.

He first provides his readers with details regarding the history of the rebel colony/camp on the frontier. According to Hunter 'the rebel camp on the Punjab frontier owes its origin to Sayyid Ahmad',[9] (4) one of the many Muslims, in Hunter's view, who turned to warfare because of punitive British policies. Hunter cannot give Sayyid Ahmad the agency to decide on his own the mode of Muslim resistance to the British, but must place it within the larger structure of failed British policies, for only then can he propose a solution to the Muslim question. Hunter then relates a brief history of Sayyid Ahmad's war with the British and the Sikhs. Hunter also mentions the parallel system of government and tax collection instituted by the rebel leader and how this system became a self-sustaining movement after Sayyid Ahmad's death in 1831. Hunter explains the continuation of Sayyid Ahmad's rebellion:

> The prophet [Sayyid Ahmad] had established a regular system of apostolic successors, both in our territory and upon the Sikh Frontier. The movement was thus placed beyond the contingencies of the life or death of any of the individual leaders, and his own decease had been converted by the zeal of his followers into an apotheosis for the further spread of the faith. (13)

It seems quite obvious that the rebel camp on the frontier was set up to surpass the constraints of time and space. By spreading its support base all over British India, it could transcend time through continuity. What Hunter invokes here is a perpetual state of war in the frontier with growing support within the Indian heartland, unless some drastic steps are taken. In a sense, what this state of affairs seems to suggest is that this particular problem has the potential to be popularised and generalised and can only be addressed through wide-ranging reforms in administering the Muslim population of India.

The second chapter, aptly titled 'The Chronic Conspiracy within our Territory' focuses on the problem of material support to the rebels from within the British territories. Here, Hunter also links Sayyid Ahmad's movement with the global Wahabi revival. By connecting Indian rebels with the Wahabis, Hunter achieves a strategic advantage: his narrative links the Indian uprising to a term that was hardly unknown to the British, for they had encountered Wahabi movements elsewhere too. This rhetorical move places the Indian Muslim movement within both pre-existing myths and historical realities of the British encounters with the Wahabis. Thus, the term Wahabi, in itself, carries a meaning beyond the literal meaning of the word or its explanation; it becomes a metaphor for the kind of native threat and fanaticism that the British had faced elsewhere in the British Empire. Hunter, while tracing the development of Sayyid Ahmad, makes this connection obvious and suggests: 'Until his pilgrimage to Mecca, however, he does not appear to have reduced his doctrines to any formulated system, (45) which clearly links Sayyid Ahmad with the global influence of the Wahabi movement of Arabia.[10]

Hunter's account of the first Wahabi trial is the most important aspect of his second chapter. This is also where Ja'far Thanesari's account becomes pertinent to my inquiry, for he is one of the defendants mentioned in Hunter's account. We now learn about the specific historical personalities caught in the local web of Muslim conspiracy, which Hunter has already placed in its broader historical and geographical context.

Ja'far, we are told, was converted by Yahya Ali of Patna, the 'Spiritual Director of the Wahabi sect in India' (82). As a result of this conversion Ja'far 'devoted much time to self-examination, and rigidly kept account with his soul' (80). Hunter also provides us with an excerpt from Ja'far's diary used as evidence against him in court. This excerpt represents Ja'far's self-view from within the British-run court system (in which he was a scrivener). Hunter quotes: 'The mere contact with the Musalman employees of the Unbeliever, which was the drawback attending my position, acted as a poison to my soul' (81). Hence, through his own admission to Hunter, Ja'far ceases to be an individual and becomes a quintessential Muslim subject struggling with the deep existential dilemma of functioning within a political system run by unbelievers. Even Ja'far's turn to religious dispensations of Yahya Ali is caused by a duality of loyalties to his workplace. What Hunter foregrounds in this passage, then, are the general aspects of Muslim anxieties of negotiating the new power structure, in which even their material successes could not obviate the deep anxieties of day-to-day contact with non-Muslims. A person like this must work to change such a system that is poison to his soul. About Yahya Ali, Hunter quotes the final statement by the judge before he announced his death sentence:

> He is a highly educated man, who can plead no excuse of ignorance. What he has done, he has done with forethought, resolution, and the bitterest treason.... He aspires to the merit of a religious reformer; but instead of appealing to

reason he seeks his end in political revolution, and madly plots against the government, which probably saved the Muhammadans of India from extinction, and certainly brought religious freedom. (85)

It is obvious from these concluding remarks that, as opposed to Hindu reformers, Yahya Ali is held accountable for politicizing his reform movement. If his reforms had stayed within the realm of the social, he would not have become a threat to the raj. It is, therefore, the very political nature of his activities that makes him a threat to the British system. On the other hand, we have already learned from Ja'far's journal [cited above] that for a Muslim of faith, the mere contact with a non-Muslim power, despite the material advantages, was a contaminating experience, making it imperative for the Muslims to work towards changing the political order. Therefore, the Muslim response to the British is within the political domain and cannot be read only within the social. Ja'far's account of the events gives us the native version of the same story. He begins with an account of the circumstances of his arrest:[11]

> Towards the end of 1863 a great war began near the western border of India due to the heavy-handedness of the British government....All the armies from the Punjab cantonments were thrown into this conflict....In such a sensitive situation, on 11 December 1863, a Vilayti Afghan police officer named Ghazan Khan, who was stationed at Pani Pat Police Post of District Karnal, found out some information about me and for his worldly gain sent a fallacious report about me to the Deputy Commissioner of Karnal. The report stated that the Numberdar of Thanesar, Muhammad Ja'far, was aiding the Mujahideen with money and manpower. (27-28)

Thus, from the very outset Ja'far places his story within the larger structure of the Muslim struggle against the British and the treason of one particular Muslim that results in his arrest. In his account of the arrest, though, Ja'far does not claim innocence; he is not embroiled in a false court case. Rather, he has been aiding the jihad, but that does not make the actions of a fellow Muslim less reprehensible. Thus, when the police come to search his house, he is worried about the letter that includes 'instructions to the caravan leader informing him about the dispatch of a few thousand gold coins' (29). The narrative follows his escape and eventual arrest at Aligarh. He then informs us of his torture and beating and the final offer by the British officers (a policy that Hunter deems effective). The British officials tell him: 'if you inform us of the other participants of the Jihad, we will make you a state witness and give you a prestigious job; if you choose otherwise you will be hanged' (37), an offer which Ja'far refuses.

In Thanesari's account, the irrationality of the Wahabi fanatics is rearticulated as a rational, defiant response to the British. Thanesari's account of his incarceration, along with Yahya Ali and others, tells us the inside story of the dreams, motives and desires of the fanatics themselves; while also detailing the web of lateral goodwill and kindness between the prisoners and their native jailors. The most interesting part of Thanesari's account is his two references to Hunter's work, especially the hyperbole inherent in Hunter's representation of the Wahabi threat. Thanesari writes:

> Some selfish people have convinced our brave and wise government of the threat posed to it by us, a few hundred dervishes. One can find evidence of this in Dr Hunter's book *The Indian Musalmans*, which has made a rope into a snake and has tried to prove the presence of a wide gulf between the conquerors and the conquered. This book is entirely untrustworthy. In fact, when it was published Maulvy Sayyid Ahmad[12] logically refuted all claims of this false doctor, but for the English, this book still acts as a charm in forming their views of the Wahabis. (41)

Here, Thanesari's text becomes a part of the larger debate between the English and the Muslim elite about the question of Muslim loyalty. Thanesari further asserts the particularities of Muslim actions during the rebellion by giving the same example as everyone else, which was: that of aiding the helpless British during the rebellion. Hence, it seems that through these accounts, a discourse of Muslim representation emerges in the Muslim politics of India, which I have, for want of a better term, called Muslim exceptionalism.

Thanesari's account of Maulana Yahya Ali is also instructive for the kind of solidarity that existed amongst the prisoners during the trial. He writes:

> Maulana Yahya Ali's company was nothing less than a treasure....When I compared my own *kam-ilmi* (lack of knowledge) with such gifts of God, it felt as if a *chumar* (lowly man) had been made a king' (46).

On the other hand, Maulana Yahya Ali himself was quite ecstatic, constantly humming these verses:

> Being a Muslim I am carefree of how I am killed
> For it is to God that I shall return (46).

What is important in this narrative is the very nature of Muslim resistance. Just as the British are attempting to stamp out the rebellion; the incarcerated leaders by their imprisonment, it seems, are making new converts and creating new mythologies of resistance. What this points to is a particular Wahabi solidarity, which can later be mobilised to enhance the level of Muslim solidarity across the sectarian divide.

It is also interesting to compare the two separate accounts of the trial. I will conclude with comparing Hunter's rendition of the final trial verdicts with Thanesari's musings that he recorded after his conviction. Thanesari places his own and his colleagues' eventual persecution within the larger framework of the history of Muslim persecution at the hands of their other oppressors. Hence, what might happen to him and Yahya Ali is something akin to what happened to a famous companion of the prophet, Hazrat Habib, 'who when about to be hanged by the Quresh of Mecca died while reciting the same verses' as the ones Maulana Yahya Ali frequently recited in prison. Thanesari also places his plight within the framework of the immediate history of Muslim resistance, for he informs us that Maulana Yahya Ali also frequently remembered Sayyid Ahmad Shahid by reciting the following verses of Mir Dard:[13]

> Pass this message of Dard, when the wind passes through the abode of the beloved
> What night shall you alight, we have been waiting all these days (47).

A comparative analysis of the statements about the sentencing announcements is quite instructive in plotting the two separate ways of representing the same reality. Hunter articulates Ja'far Thanesari's statement as follows:

> It is impossible to exceed the bitter hostility, treasonable activity, and mischievous ability of this prisoner. He is an educated man and a Headman in his village. There is no doubt of his guilt and no palliation of it. (82)

Thanesari records his own sentencing verdict as follows:

> You are a wise, educated numberdar of your village. You spent all your wisdom and legal know-how in opposition to the government. Through you, money and manpower was passed to the enemies of the government. You never attempted to support the government in this process, for which you are to be hanged, your property will be confiscated, and even your body shall not be

given to your family but will be buried unceremoniously in the jail graveyard. I will be pleased to see you hang. (51)

Thanesari 'heard this verdict calmly' (51), and in response to the judge's last sentence said: 'It is in God's hands to give or take life, not in yours; it is possible that he may kill you before I am killed' (51). Thanesari informs his readers that he was 'so pleased at hearing the death sentence... as if the paradise was right in front of me' (51-2), and that 'people were crying profusely upon hearing the verdict' (52), making the event a matter of popular myth instead of merely being a tale of treason and justice, as Hunter tends to represent it.

Thanesari's account is also instructive about the interactive strategies of the prisoners as opposed to British attempts at converting people into becoming state witnesses. For example, in the case of Maulana Ahmadullah, another Wahabi leader transported to the Andaman Islands, British authorities tried to get an implicating testimony from the Wahabi prisoners already in prison. He explains the British efforts regarding the arrest of the Maulana:

> The days when our appeal was pending in the chief court of Punjab...we were informed that if we are not freed, then the British intended to arrest Maulana Ahmadullah. So when our appeal was rejected, the British attempted to turn us into false state witnesses....We told our colleagues that even though our world had been destroyed, all we had left was our faith; so let us not destroy that by becoming false state witnesses. The British might have succeeded in working on the others; but we were able to dispel that influence in our own time....Consequently Maulana Yahya Ali and I were soon transferred to the Central Jail in Lahore. And as soon as we left, Muhammad Shafi and Abdul Kareem took over the role of state-witness. As a result, in May 1865, the *wali* (guide) of his times; the sun of Islam, Hazrat Maulana Ahmadullah *sahib*, was deported to Andaman. (63-4)

The primary message that is communicated in this account is that no matter how harsh the treatment, the prisoners did maintain a certain degree of solidarity, and that they were quite capable of understanding the ramifications of their statements and actions. As such, what to Hunter seems a group of fanatical mullahs, in fact, is actually a group of extremely religious but obviously pragmatic rebels. This solidarity remains intact even during the years of exile. When Thanesari is himself transported to Andaman in 1865 one of the people he meets there is the same Maulvi Ahmadullah. Thanesari informs us that 'Maulana Ahmad Ullah was staying at Andaman's Chief Commissioner's house' (77) where they were taken to meet other friends and attend a welcoming feast. Thus, it seems that the costly trial might banish the Wahabi leaders, but it fails to silence them or to break their lateral solidarity. Some of these leaders never return from Andaman, but those who do, result in becoming the very symbols of Wahabi resistance to the British.

This dual reading of Hunter and one of the subjects in his narrative shows us two sides of the Wahabi story, but Hunter's narrative needs further attention, especially the final chapter regarding the possibilities of creating a British hegemony. I will now discuss this part of Hunter's representation while interfacing it with Sayyid Ahmad Khan's review of his book.

In Chapter 4 of the book, before putting forth his final recommendations, Hunter dwells upon the juridical opinions of the Muslim *ulama* (scholars) from the four major schools of Islamic jurisprudence. All four *fatwas* (decrees) make it imperative for Muslims to obey the government under which they live, which gives a justification for British power through divine sanctions from the sacred texts of Islam itself. However, the *fatwas* are juridical injunctions and not precepts of faith, and are, because of their contractual nature, open to interpretation. Hunter accepts that British relations with the Muslims depend upon maintaining this contract; the burden of responsibility, therefore, shifts to the government, making the Muslim question central to the British administration. The Muslims, it seems, are the Sphinx whose riddle the British must answer in order to establish some manner of hegemony, for the rebel camp still exists on that terrible Frontier, and under different circumstances, may mobilise the entire Muslim population against the British.

In Chapter Three, Hunter gives an account of several *fatwas* by major religious authorities and also gives a specific account of the Wahabi view. He then proceeds to generalise from the Wahabi perception of British authority to foresee the eventual response of Indian Muslims if the *status quo* is maintained. Hunter suggests that 'the presence of Wahabis in a District is a standing menace to all classes, whether Musalman or Hindu' (100) as they act as 'destroyers in the spirit of Robespierre or Tanchelin of Antwerp' (100). Hunter then explains the *fatwas* against a state-of-war issued by non-Wahabi *ulama* including 'three high priests at Mecca' (106) to enhance the particularity of the Wahabi case; but this particularity soon collapses into a generalised view of the Indian Musalmans. But Hunter does dwell a little on the possibility of troubles for the British if such verdicts had turned against their rule in India:

The mere fact of the question having been raised at all, reveals the perilous ground upon which our supremacy in India is based; for it should never be forgotten that such Decisions, which opposed to the government, [sic] have given rise to some of the most obstinate and bloody revolts that the world has seen. (107)

Hence, Hunter emphasizes the contractual nature of British supremacy in India; for as long as doctors of Islam see the British as fulfilling their contract as rulers, the Muslims need not rise against them to fulfil their sacred duty: however, a popular perception of injustice coupled with the divine sanction through the voices of the *ulama*, could clearly make the British position in India untenable. There is, therefore, a need to contain the Wahabis and to include the Muslims within the hegemonic project of the empire for the empire to sustain itself.

Hunter explains this tendency towards a more generalised Muslim rebellion within the possible permutations of defining the classical Muslim concepts of *Dar-ul-Harb* (Abode of War) and *Daru-ul-Islam* (Abode of Peace). It is the possibility of the fluidity of these two concepts that, Hunter fears, might escalate the tensions between the British and their Muslim subjects. He then cites the three mandatory conditions for the declaration of a country as *Dar-ul-Harb* as expounded by Maulvi Abdul Haq, who had declared that India had not yet become an abode of war:[14]

1. When the rule of the infidels is openly exercised and the *ordinances of Islam are not observed*.
2. When it is in such contiguity to a country which is *Dar-ul-Harb*, that no city of *Dar-ul-Islam* intervenes between that country and *Dar-ul-Harb*.
3. That no Musalman is found in enjoyment of religious liberty, nor a *Zimmi* (an infidel who accepted the terms of permanent subjection to Muslim rule) under the same terms as he enjoyed under the government of Islam. (118)

From his juxtaposition of a current and a classical definition of the *Dar-ul-Harb*, Hunter can now assert the importance of controlling the language of power. His above explanation clarifies to the British that unless something is done, the balance of their power hinges on the interpretation of *Dar-ul-Harb* that could be popularised and generalised for the mobilisation of Muslims. He then attributes this classical and more orthodox interpretation of the *Sharia* (Islamic law) about *Dar-ul-Harb* to the Wahabis who assert that 'India has become a Country of the Enemy [Abode of War], and from this they deduce the obligation of *Jihad* (Holy War) against its rulers' (122). Hunter's analysis of the Muslim–British relationship is also based on the interpretation of the term *Aman-i-Awwal*, which is inextricably linked with the concept of *Dar-ul-Harb*, and hence, to an eventual general transition to a state of jihad. Hunter explains:

> *Aman* literally signifies *security*, and the meaning of *Aman-i-Aawwal* is distinctly laid down…as implying the whole religious security and full status which the Mohammedans *formerly* enjoyed under their own Rule (120).

What this implies is that the Muslim response to the British is deeply embedded in their view of the India of the present, and if, somehow, the Muslims could convince themselves that the contract of the *Aman-i-Awwal* had been breached, then there would be no stopping the Muslim transition into an open jihad against the so-called infidels. Hunter goes on to suggest that this aspect of the *Aman-i-Awwal* was already in breach for the 'Aman, or religious status, which the Muhammadans now enjoy, is entirely dependent on the will of their Christian rulers' (120).

Hence, the problem tends to be a question of containment: can the Muslims be convinced that the contract of *Aman* between them and their English rulers is still intact, even though, according to Hunter, it is already in *de facto* breach? Hunter goes on to claim that the majority of Muslims would not rebel for as long as they have the minimum level of *aman* available. To maintain peace, Hunter suggests, the Muslims do not need 'their former complete status under Muhammadan Rule, but sufficient provisions for the protection of their lives, and property, and the safety of their souls' (132). One may assume from this statement that the Muslims are unlikely to slide into a general rebellion if the government maintains the least amount of its contractual responsibilities, which still makes this relationship more hegemonic than that of brute dominance. Hunter also suggests that under the present conditions, 'the present generation of Musalmans are bound, according to their own texts, to accept the *status quo*' (132). But this *status quo* can only be maintained if 'the British maintain their end of the contract as rulers, and not interfere in Muslim religious affairs' (133). Hence, Hunter, through his long exegesis, reaches the conclusion that the nature of Muslim–British relationship is contractual. His conclusion highlights the importance of the consent of the governed, and the fact that this contract will remain effective for as long as the British honour their end of the contract. This places the responsibility for any future engagement between the British and the Muslims entirely upon the British government; while also emphasizing the centrality of the Muslim question to the British administration of India. This analysis takes Hunter to the final chapter of his book, where he streamlines certain policies for the British government. Hunter begins the final chapter of his book with the following declaration of the British–Muslim relationship:

> The Indian Musalmans, therefore, are bound by their own law to live peacefully under our Rule. But the obligation continues only so long as we perform our share of the contract, and respect their rights and spiritual privileges. Once let us interfere with their civil and religious status (*Aman*)... and their duty to us ceases. We may enforce submission, but we can no longer claim obedience. (138)

What Hunter describes in the beginning of his final chapter is the core of British administrative doctrine, and it makes dealing with the Muslim question central to the very existence of the raj. This is also the reason, as opposed to Ranjit Guha's claims,[15] the British liberal project cannot completely wipe out what Guha considers the pre-capitalist and feudal mode of production, for that would require a complete erasure of religion from the discourse of colonialism. In Hunter's view, however, religion can be used while creating British hegemony, but only if the sense of Muslim particularity and the sanctity of the basic tenets of their faith are maintained.

Hunter goes on to criticise the wrongdoings of British policies and suggests that incarcerating or transporting the 'ringleaders' of the conspiracy is one possible solution, but the best way of fighting the conspiracy is, 'by detaching from it the sympathies of the general Muhammadan community' (140), which, he asserts, can only be accomplished by 'removing the chronic sense of wrong which has grown up in the hearts of the Musalmans under British Rule' (140). As Hunter has already established that this state of Muslim resistance could be generalised under the present conditions, he now suggests a strategic approach to creating and maintaining British hegemony over the Muslims.

As a first step, Hunter suggests, a cleavage must be created between the popular and the religious elite, and that, he argues, can only be achieved through a hegemonic process and not through dominance alone. Thus, Hunter forces his British audience to think strategically about the

Muslim question, and then suggests long-term measures that involve administrative and not just militaristic approaches to it. Also, having established the fact that it is not religion that is the cause of the Muslim perpetual opposition to the British, he goes on to secularise the Muslim problem by shifting the focus from the religious to the material causes of the Muslim distrust of the British. Hence, God is written out of the Muslim negotiation of power and replaced by a liberal rational approach to the problems of power. Hunter lists the Muslim grievances as follows:

> They accuse us of having closed every honourable walk of life to professors of their creed. They accuse us of having introduced a system of education which leaves their whole community unprovided for....They accuse us of having brought misery into thousands of families, by abolishing their law officers. (140)

Hunter then goes on to trace the impact of the British takeover on the fortunes of the Bengal Muslim nobility, on the Muslim law doctors and on the Muslim physicians. On the plane of sentiment, he suggests that the Muslims accuse the British of having 'shown no pity in the time of our triumph' (141). Through his analysis of the Muslim situation in Bengal, a narrative of general Muslim misery and distrust of the British emerges, a narrative now based on the detailed analysis of a British subject, an Orientalist, who knows his subjects better than most British government functionaries. And since the aim is to ensure the stability of the raj, Hunter can now offer his long-term solution to the Muslim question: education and vertical mobility for the Muslims. Hence, the attempt is to incorporate the Muslim youth within the British system in order to build a hegemonic rather than a dominant relationship.

Even though what Hunter suggests in his book is not so different from what Sayyid Ahmad Khan had highlighted in his earlier work, *The Causes of the Indian Rebellion*, Sayyid responds to Hunter's book with a deeply critical review. To understand Sir Sayyid's response one must keep in mind his general strategy in negotiating with the British power. Since his mission, in Aziz Ahmad's words, 'had been to salvage the wreck of his community on the raft of loyalism' (125), he must condemn any work that attempts to challenge the Muslim claim to loyalty. Sir Sayyid attacks the generalisability of Hunter's work first:

> Dr Hunter expressly states that it is only the Bengal Mohammedans to whom he applies the subject-matter of the book, and that it is only them whom he

knows intimately. The book, however, abounds in passages which lead the
reader to believe that it is not merely the Bengal Mohammedans that the
author treats of, but the Mohammedans throughout India. (67)

This tendency to generalise Muslim feelings towards the British is
certainly an anathema to Sayyid Ahmad's whole project: proving that
Muslims can be good British subjects and that the rebellion—as we have
already discussed—was caused by special circumstances. Sir Sayyid's
strategic goal here is to challenge the very nature of the act of
representation itself. His concern is not only about how the British
represent the Muslims; but how a representation by a British official feeds
into the Muslim distrust of British intentions? He suggests, 'what books
and newspapers enunciate is, by the general native public, believed to be
the opinion of the whole English community' (66). Under such
circumstances a 'misrepresentation' (66) of Muslim reality can only hurt
the British attempts at creating a more loyal Muslim public. Loyalist he
may be, but Sir Sayyid is unapologetic when it comes to controlling the
borders of Muslim representation, and such acts, as we saw in Thanesari's
reference to this particular review, make him a champion of the Muslim
cause. Thus, this review does not only defend the sanctity of Muslim
representation, but it also serves as a medium of popular legitimacy for
Sayyid Ahmad Khan. Sir Sayyid then devotes a considerable amount of
time in defining the Wahabi sect of Islam and in suggesting that the hill
tribes, that Hunter lumps together with the Wahabis, are not Wahabi at
all but rather strict Hanafis. Finally, in his concluding remarks he
challenges Hunter's views about the possibility of Muslim loyalty to the
British:

> Towards the end of the third chapter, Dr Hunter says that he has no hope of
> enthusiastic loyalty and friendship from the Mohammedans of India; the
> utmost he can expect from them is a cold acquiescence in British rule. If our
> author is so hopeless on account of our faith being that of Islam, let me
> commend to his attention the 85th verse, chapter V of the Holy Koran
> (George Sale's Translation): 'Thou shalt surely find the most violent of all men
> in enmity against the true believers [Muslims] to be the Jews and the idolaters;
> and thou shalt surely find those among them to be the most inclined to
> entertain friendship from true believers who say we are Christians. (81)

This particular reference from the Qur'an presents a predisposed Muslim
view of Christians, for even the Qur'an attests that they could be friends
with Muslims. In Sir Sayyid's view, then, there is no scriptural reason for

Muslims to distrust their Christian rulers. As Hunter's book saw religious duty of all Muslims to rebel against British authority; Sir Sayyid, therefore, finds a justification for a just Muslim–Christian relationship in the holiest sources of Islamic jurisprudence, the Qur'an. He goes on to argue that as long as Muslims could freely practice their religion under the British, they had no reason to rebel against the latter.

This brief discussion illustrates the nature of post-Rebellion textual production. While Sayyid Ahmad and his cohorts remain loyalists to the very end, this loyalty is normalised in the name of the people. In this process of defending the representation of Muslims, the idea of Muslim particularity takes shape, for unless the Muslims are able to present their case as separate and particular, the project of post-rebellion Muslim rehabilitation cannot be completed. Sayyid Ahmad Khan goes on to establish a Muslim university[16] that eventually provides leadership for Muslim nationalist politics. But political texts were not the only textual production of the loyalist school. In his life Sayyid Ahmad Khan was also able to influence some leading Muslim poets, writers, and scholars. It is to their literary production that I will turn to in the next two chapters.

NOTES

1. During the rebellion, Sayyid Ahmad Khan was stationed at Bijnaur where his efforts saved the lives of two resident European families. Hali includes a detailed account of this in *Hayat-i-Javed* 69-96.
2. This, of course, is in my translation. The Urdu text translated here is cited from the same book that includes the English version, it being a bilingual volume.
3. The main clause of the law prohibited any forfeiture of property if a person changed his/her religion: 'Law or usage which inflicts forfeiture of, or affects, rights on change of religion or loss of caste to cease to be enforced.' Muslims saw this law as an encouragement by the British government for low caste Hindus to convert to Christianity. The full text of the Act XXI of 1850 can be accessed online: http://indianchristians.in/news/images/resources/pdf/caste_disabilities_removal_act_1850.pdf, accessed 20 February 2009.
4. Popularly called the Widow Remarriage Act, this law made it illegal for anyone to forcibly stop a widow from remarrying. The law was especially designed to curtail the upper caste Hindu practice of enforced widowhood.
5. For a detailed account of the Mughal land revenue system see Dr P. Saran's work on the subject.
6. All citations from this text are in my translation.
7. For a detailed analysis of the Great Wahabi Trial see A.G. Noorani, 93-113.
8. In postcolonial theory Ariel and Caliban signify two specific native colonial subjectivities: Ariel connotes the native who has been co-opted by the colonising master while Caliban represents the resistant native. For a detailed theoretical account of these two tropes of native subjectivity see Chinweizu.

9. For the most authoritative history of Sayyid Ahmad Shahid's rebellion see Ghulam Rasul Mehr's Urdu work on the subject.

10. Within the same chapter Hunter also gives his readers a brief explanation of the Wahabi movement and the chief tenets of the Wahabi sect as stipulated by Abdul Wahab, the founder of the Wahabi sect of Islam.

11. *Kala Pani* was published during the British Raj and the author, therefore, is quite careful in representing the facts of the story. His attempt, throughout the story, is to provide a narrative aimed at assuring the British about the sincerity and benign nature of the Wahabi movement. The narrative is, therefore, torn between its Muslim and British audiences. The editors of this particular edition, however, have declared openly that they are publishing this work to remind the Muslim youth about the sacrifices and trials of the early Muslim heroes, and in their narrative Guantanamo is yet another Kala Pani, especially since most of the people incarcerated there happen to be from the Wahabi sect of Islam.

12. A reference to Sayyid Ahmad Khan's review of Hunter's book.

13. This is a reference to Khwajah Mir Dard (AD 1720-1785), one of the major mystic poets of his time. For details see Zaidi, 95-7.

14. Hunter juxtaposes Abdul Hakk's *fatwa*, derived from *Fatawa-i-Alamgiri*, with the classical definition of the concept as explained by Imam Abu Hanifa in his *Sirajiyah Imaddiya*, which incidentally is a more stringent and confining definition of the concept and which if invoked would immediately transform India into the Abode of War.

15. I discuss this in more detail in Chapter 4.

16. For the purpose of brevity I will not be discussing the rise of Aligarh Muslim University. Major scholars of India and Pakistan, however, have covered the subject quite extensively. David Lelyved's *Aligarh's First Generation* is a good book on this particular aspect of Sayyid Ahmad Khan's career.

3

The Muslim Literary Renaissance: Muhammad Hussain Azad and Altaf Hussain Hali

Considering Altaf Hussain Hali (1837–1914) and Muhammad Hussain Azad (1835–1910) as the two architects of the post-rebellion Muslim literary 'reconstruction', Francis Pritchett presents the following view of their circumstances immediately after the rebellion:

> The process of reconstruction had to start with basic, pragmatic concerns: finding a job, finding a way to live in the new world. In the years immediately following the Rebellion, Azad and Hali had to cut their coats according to their cloth. And since India was now to belong directly to queen-empress, it was more and more clear that the only cloth available would be imported fabric. (31)

Pritchett is suggesting here that the political order had altered drastically after the rebellion, and it was in this political scenario that the two architects of the post-rebellion literary renaissance functioned: deeply traumatized by the rebellion and its aftermath and greatly worried about the loss of Urdu poetic tradition and along with it the possibility of the future of Urdu literature. Hence, they both, Pritchett suggests, changed the course of Urdu letters from romance tradition to realism, or what they termed *nacher* (nature) poetry. It is this realistic imperative that, in due course, serves the great function of highlighting Muslim particularity and exceptionalism. After Hali and Azad's intervention, Urdu literature becomes synonymous with Muslim literature and its utilitarian emphasis forces future writers to write *to and for* the Muslims of India and about the Muslim existential dilemmas within the British system. The main focus of my discussion in this chapter is to trace the shift in Urdu literature from the detached formalism of pre-rebellion literary production to a more popular, utilitarian, and didactic form. I will start with a brief discussion of Azad's *Aab-e-Hayaat*[1] (Water of Life) and then discuss Altaf Hussain Hali's work in greater detail.

Azad was 27 at the time of the rebellion. The British executed his father, Maulvi Muhammad Baqir, for his journalistic activities during the rebellion, and Azad fled to Lahore after Delhi fell to the British (Pritchett 22-23). Hence, Azad saw the death of one order and the ascendancy of another. The rebellion marked for him both a personal and a collective loss. *Aab-e-Hayaat* was, therefore, his attempt at saving a vanishing tradition, but in doing so the text itself became a canonical text about the literary achievements of Muslims within the bound pages of one volume. Hence, besides serving as an archive of the Muslim past, it also became a monument for future generations. Azad's purpose in compiling this work was not just aesthetic or literary; as a leading figure of post-rebellion Muslim letters, he also wanted the text to instil pride of accomplishment and literary education in a generation that had lost control of its culture and its political systems of support. *Aab-e-Hayaat*, therefore, is a particularly didactic Muslim text. In the preface, Azad provides the following reasons for his project:[2]

> My friends, life is not just eating, drinking, walking, talking and sleeping. Life's real meaning lies in one's popularity and immortality of the qualities associated with one's name. Now, isn't it sad that our ancestors, who possessed good qualities and passed them down to us, should be forgotten....Witnessing the events of the lives of these elders makes them alive to us, teaches us to walk the complex paths of life, and instructs us to make our lives equally as useful. Furthermore, our newly educated youth, whose minds are enlightened by English lanterns, object to the inaccuracies of our *Tazkiras*.[3] Our old writers did not commit everything to writing; they considered the minor details a matter of conversation amongst friends. They, therefore, were not aware of the importance of such minutae. They did not know that the leaf of time will turn, old families will be destroyed, and their progeny will become so ignorant as to forget the histories of their own families. And if someone tells them of the things about their own family, they ask for proof. It is these things that have made it imperative on me that, as far as possible, I should gather all that I know or find in scattered *Tazkiras* about our ancestors and commit it to writing so that their live images manifest themselves in front of us; so that they may find everlasting life. (7-8)

The above account clarifies the two main causes for Azad's project: preservation of the works of his literary ancestors and provision of living role models for the British-educated youth. Rich in its recording of famous anecdotes and questionable events about the lives of great Muslim poets, *Aab-e-Hayaat* transcends its cultural emphasis by preserving and publicizing cultural knowledge to the youth. Writing about the importance of Azad's *Aab-e-Hayaat*, Francis Pritchett concludes her chapter on Azad in the following words:

> *Water of Life* is built up from fragments of the old lost world, painstakingly reordered and rearranged in Azad's mind and heart. No one could argue that Azad's anecdotes are historically accurate....But if the parts are flawed, the whole vision is nevertheless persuasive—and in its essentials true to the world it seeks to depict. Azad shows us the classical ustad in his glory—lord of the world of speech, ruler of the imagination. (59)

What is instructive about Pritchett's concluding remarks about Azad's accomplishment is its iconic and didactic function. Through his work, Azad does not only preserve what could have been a lost tradition, but also becomes an icon for a new age of poetry, a poetry more public, more particular, and more in tune with the changed times. It is this aspect of Azad's work that impacts the later literary production of the Muslim literary elite: the marriage between the poet and his immediate audience, and the inherent public and political nature of this relationship. Ali Jawad Zaidi captures Azad's public role in the following words:

> Azad had himself studied at Delhi College and a subtle perception of change seems to have coloured his thinking. One can sense it in some of his earlier poems but it was not until he reached Lahore that his views on new poetry crystallized and he shared them with his countrymen and fellow writers....(276)

These views on new poetry are quite obviously utilitarian and suggest poetry of a more public kind, for Azad insisted that 'it was the function of the poetry to brighten up man's life and his surroundings' (Zaidi 276). This shift of poetry from the interiority and high diction of Ghalib's time to a more public function was an outcome of the material circumstances following the 1857 Rebellion. Zaidi also traces the impact of Azad's changed stance on the role of poetry in the public *mushairahs* (poetic gatherings) convened by Azad after 'the establishment of Anjuman-e-Punjab in 1874' (276). What we see in this shift is that poetry now becomes public practice through the institution of the *mushairahs* and their chosen topics are more concerned with real-life issues rather than affairs of the heart that were a characteristic aspect of classical Urdu poetry. For Azad and his followers, then, Urdu poetry could only be meaningful if it served a public function, and it is in this new emphasis on the public utility of art that the idea of Muslim exceptionalism is articulated within the literary realm. According to Dr Saleem Akhtar[4] the Anjuman-e-Punjab, established by the Punjab Government on 21 January 1865, espoused the following five goals:

1. Renaissance of classical Eastern knowledge, and encouragement of the study of languages, ethnography, history, and the ancient sites of India and neighbouring countries.
2. Spread of public education through native languages.
3. Development of trade and industry.
4. Propagating a dialogue on social, literary, scientific, and political topics; explaining public good works of the government; enhancing national loyalty and citizenship of a common state, and advising the government about the wishes and demands of the people.
5. In all aspects of public welfare, bringing the government officials and the educated and notable people of the province together. (348-349)

It is quite obvious from its stipulated missions that the Anjuman was mainly a public forum, and within its public function, it was established to provide a sort of legitimation for the Punjab government. But it is precisely within this public nature of the Anjuman that the popular function of Urdu literature is articulated in the form of *mushairahs* organized by the Anjuman. Out of all the functions, Azad, of course, was most actively engaged in its cultural aspect of which the annual *mushairahs* were the most important. These *mushairahs*, suggests Dr Saleem Akhtar, 'launched Romanticism in Urdu poetry and provided a venue for the Urdu poem' (350).[5] The Anjuman organized ten *mushairahs*, out of which seven were held in 1874 and three in 1875. Some of the topics chosen for these *mushairahs* are quite instructive in terms of the public function that they sought to achieve, such as: *Barsaat* (rainy season); *Aman* (peace); *ummeed* (hope); *Hubb-e-Watan* (patriotism); and *Tehzeeb* (civilization).

   To understand the political nature of these *mushairahs* and the politics of literary production launched by the choice of genre and topics, we must first understand their particular process and organization. A *mushairah*, in the classical Urdu sense, meant a gathering of leading poets of the time to read to a select audience their works in progress, or the works written specifically for a specially organized *mushairah*. The Anjuman *mushairahs* were different from their pre-rebellion counterparts in two respects: in the composition of the audience and the choice of poetical genre. Pre-rebellion *mushairahs* were more exclusive and were organized by the nobility; secondly, pre-rebellion *mushairahs* were mostly *ghazal* oriented and the poets were requested to compose a *ghazal* emulating the theme, metre, and rhyme scheme of a *misra-e-tarrah* (first line/verse) provided by the organizers. Hence, the previous *mushairahs* were more about the form and mastery of the convention and less about the real world. The Anjuman *mushairahs*, by focusing on the *nazm* (poem), added more immediacy to the poetical expression. Specific topics replaced the first-verse and the selected genre, the *nazm*, provided more freedom to the poets, making the poetry so composed less esoteric and more concerned with the masses. Also, as the Anjuman *mushairahs* were open to the public, they created a public event and space where all aspiring poets and all interested audiences could participate. This performance of poetry on current topics launched the public and reformative function of poetry, which also became a performative precursor of Muslim nationhood.[6] Altaf Hussain Hali, one of Azad's close companions, was amongst the poets who participated in at least three of the Anjuman *mushairahs*.

I will now move on to discuss Hali's contribution to Urdu poetry and to Muslim particularity and exceptionalism.

Hali, as Dr Saleem Akhtar informs us, was born in Panipat and had no natural ties to either the Delhi or the Lucknow School of Urdu Poetry; he was, therefore, equally at ease in critically appraising both the Schools. (337). Besides his *Diwan*, Hali is famous for his two most influential works: *Musaddas-e-Hali*[7] (1875) and *Muqaddama-e-She'r-o-Shairi* (1893). Both these works are instrumental in highlighting the particular Muslim state of being and the desired direction of Urdu poetry: poetry which is more in sync with the real, more in tune with the changed times, and more cognizant of its reformative role. In the words of Aziz Ahmad, the *Musaddas* 'was the first Urdu poem to depart from the tradition of conventionalized classicism, and it inaugurated a cultural renaissance and a vogue for political romanticism' (97). *Muqaddama-e-She'r-o-Shairi* (An Introduction to Poetry) is Hali's major contribution to the post-Rebellion direction of Urdu poetry and his *Musaddas*, besides being a good example of his theory of poetry, is the first of the major Urdu poems with a strong didactic and reformative function. I will discuss both these works, focusing on their role in articulating Muslim exceptionalism and particularity in the post-rebellion world.

Comprising 456, six-line stanzas, *Musaddas Maddo Jazr-e-Islam* (The Rise and Fall of Islam) was published in 1875 and became a popular success (Pritchett 42). As is obvious from the title, the poem explores the reasons for the rise and fall of Islam in general, and Indian Islam in particular. It is this critical approach of the poem to the general state of Muslims; and its didactic approach to the Muslims of India that qualifies the poem to be an important literary accomplishment as well as a political manifesto for Indian Muslims. Hence, even though the poem does not invoke the nation in the Western or in the traditional sense of European nationalism, it may be termed as a proto-nationalistic poem since it addresses a specifically Muslim audience. Hali, in the preface to the first edition, provides the following reasons for writing the poem:[8]

> The nation[9] is in a state of devastation; *Shurfaa* have been wiped out; knowledge is dead; and religion lives only in name. Poverty haunts every house and character has deteriorated. The clouds of prejudice are spread over the whole nation and everyone is shackled with the chains of tradition. All necks are laden with the burden of ignorance and blind obedience. The nobles, who can benefit the nation, are unaware and carefree; *Ulama*, who have the power to reform the nation, are unaware of the needs and intricacies of current times. In such circumstances one must do what one can, for as everyone is in the same boat, preserving the boat is akin to self-preservation. (8)

It is quite obvious that the *Musaddas* is a poem for the Muslim nation of India and not for a nation-state. It does not articulate the need for a separate homeland, nor does it attempt to incite a rebellion against the British, but it dwells on the causes of the downfall of Islam in India. It is this particularity of the poem—its target being a specific Muslim audience—that classifies it as a nationalistic poem. Even though Azad compares it to the 'boring flavor of chick-peas' (Pritchett 43), it articulates the very substance of the kind of reformative poetry that Azad himself expected from the Urdu poetry of his time. In the preface, Hali also points out the failure of the two potential sources of national regeneration: The *umara* (nobility) and the *ulama* (Islamic scholars). Hence, it seems, it is the callousness of the nobility, who do not understand the needs of their own people, and the ignorance of the *ulama*, who have no understanding of the new system of knowledge and power, that has made it necessary for the poet to take upon himself the task of reformation and regeneration. This task can only be accomplished by comparing the Muslim past with their present, and by making poetry more utilitarian and accessible. Hali explains further in the preface:

To the people of Delhi and Lucknow[10] this poem is like boiled rice and bland curry, but I have not written this poem for the matters of taste or to hear praise. I have written it to shame my friends [into action] and I will consider it a favour if they read and understand it, but if they don't, then that is all right too. (9)

Before I discuss the contents of the poem, it is important to glance through Hali's second preface, written for the second edition of the poem which was published six years after its initial publication. Here, Hali has the benefit of the hindsight and knowledge of the popular reception of the poem. He writes:

Musaddas Maddo Jazr-e-Islam was published in 1296 Hijra (1875). Even though its publication has not caused a great change in the society, it has, surprisingly, achieved some fame all over India in these six years. This was a completely different poem: it castigated the public and pointed out their failings; the language was used as a sword. However, in a short while this poem reached all corners of India. So far about eight editions have been published in various regions of India. In some public schools, its excerpts are taught to children; it is recited in some *Maulood Mehfils*;[11] so many people recite its stanzas and cry, while some religious leaders use it in their sermons. Even some national theatre companies have enacted some of its parts....But I take no pride in that; if the nation did not have the desire to be moved, then a thousand poems like this could have had no impact. (10-11)

What we learn from this second preface is that the poem, within six years of its publication, had become a popular success. As the poem addresses only a Muslim audience, it can, therefore, be read as a Muslim national poem; and these nationalistic aspects of the poem will become clear when the poem is discussed later. The reference to the poem's reception is extremely important. Unlike earlier poets, Hali is not concerned with the pathos of the poem and its creator but rather with the response of the public: a response that suggests that the nation—the audience—itself was primed to respond to a poem that spoke *of* them and *to* them. This shift of emphasis from the poet to the audience makes Hali's work nationalistic with an enhanced Muslim particularity: it seems that the poet, in Hali, has finally established an enduring contact with the nation. Hali is also quite consistent here with his own explanation of the public function of poetry, which he later published as *Muqaddama-e-She'r-o-Shairi*. About its reformative function, Hali suggests:

Just as poetry can evoke sensual desire, it can also be a cause for spiritual happiness. Poetry's relationship to humankind's spiritual happiness and character needs no explanation. Even though poetry may not directly impact human character, it can be justly considered an aid in character education. (110).

Hali's great poem falls clearly within the character-building function of poetry that he himself explains in his later work. This utilitarian emphasis on the role of poetry clearly transports Urdu poetry from the realm of the aesthetic to the public and political. In the first edition of the poem, Hali had only focused on the past and the present of the Muslim nation: the poem was thus pessimistic and did not offer any hope for the future. Hali, therefore, 'upon insistence of some friends' (11) included an addendum to the second edition: an addition that articulates the possibilities of some change in the future. Hence, the second edition of the poem completes the project of a public poet: to articulate the nation in the past, present, and the future. The second edition of the poem, therefore, explains the nation in three phases: the rise, the fall, and the possibility of regeneration. It is these aspects of the poem and its public political function that I will now discuss.

The poem, as included in the second edition, comprises three parts: the rise of Islam (past); the fall of Islam (present); and the hope for a future. The poem begins with a hypothetical question asked of Plato:

> Someone inquired of Plato
> What are the most dangerous ailments?
> He said there is no sickness for which God
> Has not created a cure, except when
> The patient minds not the sickness
> And considers absurd the physician's advice. (14)

This sets the stage for Hali's long poem: the Muslim body politic is sick, but their lack of desire to cure this sickness is the worst kind of ailment. The poet must, therefore, awaken this nation first just to note the existence of a problem before attempting to offer a solution. Hali further explains this state of the *qaum* (nation) in the third stanza:

> This is the state in the world of this nation
> Whose ship is caught in the whirlpool
> While the bank is far and the storm unrelenting
> The ship is about to sink in a moment

But the people on the ship show no movement
They are caught in an unaware sleep. (15)

The nation, unaware of its own ailment, is on the verge of destruction, and is unaware of an impending doom. For, as Hali says in the next stanza, they do not even know 'What they were yesterday from what they are today/For they were awake a moment ago and are now deep asleep' (15). It is this state of stupor that the poet must dispel before offering a remedy. It is important to note that Hali here uses the specific term *qaum* for nation instead of the more universal Muslim concept of *ummah*. As will become obvious, Hali uses the term *ummah* only within its pan-Islamic usage, while narrating the accomplishments of the global Muslim community; it is only in the Indian context that he uses the specific term *qaum* for the Muslims of India. But this dual usage also creates a seamless connection between the global Muslim past and its specific Indian Muslim version.

In Hali's attempt, then, the Muslims of India can only be mobilized to change their state by first putting them in touch with the larger ideological concept of *ummah*, i.e. the larger history of Islam, for only then can they visualize how far they have fallen from the zenith of Muslim accomplishments. But first I will briefly explain the concept of *ummah* and *qaum,* as these two are sometimes synonymous but often competing principles of Muslim identity:

> The Islamic concept of *Ummah* originated under the Prophet Muhammad (peace be upon him) in the seventh century of the Common Era. Those who believed in the Prophet's message and migrated from Makkah to Madinah with the Prophet formed a closely-knit group. This group later came to be known as *Ummatul Muslimin* or the *Ummah.* (Al-Ahsan 3)

Al-Ahsan also traces the usage of the term within the Qur'an, where, according to his research, the 'term occurs on 64 occasions' (9). Speaking about the usage of the term *qaum* in the Qur'an, Al-Ahsan suggests:

> The Qur'an makes a distinction between two words with similar meanings, i.e. *ummah* and *qawm*. Both words appear together....*Ummah* is used to describe a group of people who are thoroughly committed to the beliefs of the whole community (*qawm*)...*Ummah* is more specific while *Qawm* is more general. The specific quality of the *ummah* involves the ideological nature of the described. *Ummah*, therefore, means not only an ideological community but also a set of beliefs within a community, an exemplar of a community, a

more committed group of people within a community, and the lifetime of a community. (14-15)

Thus, Hali's *qaum*, the Muslims of India, even though a smaller group than the larger universal of the *ummah*, remains a general group as opposed to its more ideologically specific counterpart, the *ummah*. Hali, however, uses the term *qaum* to denote all the Muslims of India in their particularity but attempts to awaken them with references to the larger but ideologically more specific identity of the Muslim *ummah*. The Muslim idea of the nation—*qaum*—is, therefore, inherently linked with the larger ideological concept of the *ummah*: this link is so important that for Hali to awaken his *qaum*, the history of the *ummah* must first be retrieved and juxtaposed with the state of the Muslim nation of India. Hence, Hali cannot just invoke the nation in its territorial sense; the nation must come into being as part of a larger and more glorious Muslim historical community of *ummah*. Resultantly, the idea of Muslim nationhood cannot only be linked to space; it must also be articulated within its temporal structures.

The first part of the *Musaddas* dwells on the rise of Islam and Islamic civilization: Hali explains the rise of Islam in various spheres of human life over eighty-five, six-line stanzas. But before broaching the subject of the beginning of Islam, he first provides a brief overview of the time before the advent of Islam, the time termed as the *Jahiliyyah* (ignorance) period of the Arab history. The Arabia of the *Jahiliyyah* period, according to Hali, was engulfed in the following problems:

It was isolated and without a shade of civilization. (16)
It was a barren land dependent on rains. (17)
It was a land of superstition. (18)
Every tribe worshipped its own idol and the *Kaaba* was a storehouse of idols. (18)
The Arabs were divided and engaged in continuous tribal warfare. (19)
They buried their daughters alive on infancy. (20)
Drinking and gambling were favourite Arab pastimes. (20)

These are some of the ills of the *Jahiliyyah* period that Hali explains in thirteen stanzas before beginning to express the rise of Islam. It is quite obvious that this versification of the *Jahiliyyah* period draws quite heavily from the Muslim historiography about pre-Islamic Arabia. Stylistically, it sets a contrast between the world before the coming of the prophet and the positive change that his religion, Islam, introduces within Arabia.

Hence, through this juxtaposition of the worst and the best, the inherently revolutionary reformative potential of Islam is accentuated. This also sets the stage for Hali to introduce the main character—the catalyst for change—the Prophet Muhammad (PBUH):

> He who is called the Blessing amongst prophets
> He who'd fulfil the wishes of the poor
> He who'd aid the strangers in trouble
> He who'd grieve for his own and for strangers
> The helper of the poor and supporter of the weak
> Friend of the orphans and protector of the slaves. (21)

In Hali's words, Muhammad (PBUH) is sent to Arabia to change the Arabs and then the whole world. These verses clearly exemplify the universality of the Prophet's message, his attributes, and hence a universal religion. It is to this source that Hali intends to turn the gaze of his specific nation: the Muslims of India. Hali mainly focuses on the social aspects of the Prophet's message. As is obvious from the above verses, the Prophet's example is that of a person who came to change the lives of those who needed this change and who needed such revolutionary reordering of society. The religion, then, acts as a revolutionary force that must protect the weakest in a social order: the poor, the weak, the orphans and the slaves. By invoking this function of the prophet, Hali also links the history of the Muslims of India to the real-life revolutionary history of the Prophet and early Islam. Hali further explains the social and didactic aspects of the Prophet's teachings:

> He taught the poor the value of hard work
> To earn a living with their own hand
> To be able to take care of self and others
> To avoid begging from door to door
> He taught the rich that in this world
> Those who are rich and prosperous
> Must help and aid the others. (30)

These verses provide a historical precedence for the current action. As we will see later, Hali will use this knowledge to criticize the current state of the rich and poor Muslims of India. Within its historical context, this provides an example of social responsibility that the prophet's teaching introduced in early Islam. The poor are encouraged to strive and not simply wait for handouts from the rich; at the same time the rich are also encouraged to share their wealth and resources for the good of the masses. Hali, in the later part of the poem, considers this dual social responsibility an important precondition of Muslim revival.

Hali then traces the causes of the rise of Islamic civilization under several interconnected registers. The first and the foremost cause of the rise of Islam, in Hali's words, is the Muslim love for knowledge. Muslims, Hali informs his readers:

> Went to every wine shop to fill their cup
> Went to every stream to quench their thirst
> Followed every light like a moth
> They kept in sight Prophet's Instruction:
> Consider knowledge a lost treasure and
> When found, gather it unto yourself as your own. (38)

So, in Hali's view, the primary cause of the rise and success of Muslim civilization was this unquenchable and eclectic quest for knowledge. This approach to the appropriation of human knowledge is a direct challenge to the more conservative religious views of Hali's contemporaries for whom knowledge only meant the knowledge of Islamic texts. By placing the rise of Islam in this quest for the use and appropriation of human knowledge, Hali, as we will notice later, opens up a space to make his case for the acquisition of modern knowledge. Just as the earlier Muslims followed the Prophet's instructions to gather knowledge onto themselves 'as a lost treasure', Hali desires that the Muslims of India should approach the current Western knowledge with the same kind of zeal and a quest which is sanctified by the Prophet. Thus so far, from Hali's depiction of the rise of Islam, the picture that emerges is that of an egalitarian, just, and inquisitive socio-political order that does not fear the new, and is not constricted by an ossified traditional view of the world.

After explaining the causes of the rise of Islamic civilization, Hali then moves on to its downward spiral, and in the process, also highlights the current troubles of the Muslims of India. But first, a brief look at the fall of the larger Islamic civilization:

> But when the fountain of truth got muddled
> And their grip on faith got loosened
> Nor remained the shade of Huma[12] on their heads
> Then was concluded God's promise
> For He never ruins anyone, besides
> Those who ruin themselves. (49)

According to Hali, this is the main cause of the fall of Islam: they had lost touch with their faith which was what made them and what made them great, and that God on His part considered His covenant pledged with the Muslims as fulfilled with the Muslims. The last two verses, however, clearly lay the burden of responsibility on the Muslims themselves, for God does not diminish a people's honour and prestige unless they themselves give up striving. Hence, the responsibility for the loss of power of Islamic civilization lies with the Muslims themselves who had lost their grip on all that made them great. This is Hali's summation of the fall of the *ummah*; from here on he particularizes the chief characteristics of the Muslims of India, which is a movement from the larger Muslim universal to the national aspects of Indian Muslim history. It is important to note that this particular community is not only Indian; but the past history that Hali has just narrated connects them with the historical concept of *ummah*. The Muslim identity is, therefore, inherently transnational as its source and its greatest achievements belong to the supranational political and ideological system of *ummah*.

In the rest of the poem, Hali focuses on tracing the causes of the fall of Indian Islam and the current state of the Muslims of India. It is in this part of the poem that Hali becomes a poet of the nation, and because of the poem's particular focus on the Indian Muslims, the poem becomes the first major nationalistic lament. Hali writes:

> The stable ship of the Hijazi faith
> Whose signs were expressed in the tales of the world
> That never stopped in the face of danger
> Nor did it hesitate in ferocious sea
> The one that mastered the seven oceans
> Finally sank on the banks of Ganges. (51)

This stanza clearly foregrounds the supranational origins of Indian Islam. It is the same universal system that stemmed from Hijaz—Makkah and Madinah—that, in Hali's words, met its unceremonious defeat in India. This juxtaposition of two sacred symbols—Hijaz for the Muslims and Ganges for the Hindus—is instructive, for it clearly suggests the particularity of Indian Islam as opposed to its opposing social system, Hinduism. Hali begins his critique of the Muslims of India in comparison with Europeans and Hindus. Compared to the Muslims of India the Europeans 'never get tired of hard work' (Hali 58). As far as the other 'nations' of India are concerned (which mainly means the Hindus) Hali opines:[13]

All the other great nations here are *prominent in trade* and wealth, in favour of *moving with the progress* of the world, and eager to *educate their children* and their nation. If they fall, they rise and stumble on. They *mould themselves according to every new cast* and change as the world changes; they *understand the time* and its demands. (Emphasis added, 58-59)

These are some extremely important observations. Hali is here articulating in verse what the Muslim leaders would eventually broach in terms of Muslim exceptionalism within the British system: the idea of Muslim 'backwardness' in comparison with their Hindu counterparts. Hali highlights the main points of comparative disadvantage between Muslims and Hindus in terms of material inequalities. Hali does not propose a return to a pure Islamic tradition in order to close the gap; in fact, he only elaborates on the glorious Muslim past to stress to his co-religionists the heights they had fallen from. The causes of Hindu success are all related to their successful negotiation of the new order: education, consistency, and capacity to change with the changing times. So, just as the great Muslim civilization had fallen due to its own weaknesses, the regeneration of the Indian Muslims now lies in their own hands; and this can be accomplished only if they strive, like the Hindus, to create a place for themselves within the changed order. The past, for Hali, is not meant to be a source of nostalgia, but a means to affect positive change in the present. Hali's reference to Hindus streamlines that, for the Muslims to rise again, a new understanding and more liberal negotiation of the new political order is necessary. These observations also make it clear that even at this early stage of Muslim national consciousness, Hali is looking at the plight of the Indian Muslims comparatively with their Hindu counterparts, and that this tendency to study the Muslim reality in comparative terms was not invented by the Muslim League, but preceded party politics and was inherently inscribed in the process of Muslim literary representation.

There are several areas in which Hali traces the fallen state of Muslims: superstition, ignorance, prejudice, loss of egalitarianism, and lack of interest in modern education. Hali means to highlight certain superstitious peculiarities of Indian Islam, due to Hindu influences. Superstitious practices local to Indian Islam include: raising the Prophet to the level of divinity; preferring other Muslim *imams* (leaders) over the Prophet; adhering to the cult of Sufi shrines; offering prayers at the graves of martyrs. All these practices are juxtaposed with the most important tenet of Islam: *Tauhid* (oneness of God). Hence, the primary flaw that Hali finds the Indian Muslims to be immersed in is their violation of this basic Muslim principle that stood them apart from Christians and Hindus. This was also the foremost stance of the Deoband and Barelwi Islamic reformers in India, which I will discuss later. When Hali talks of prejudice, he means a particular mode of social behaviour. The word that he uses here is *ta'ssub*, which is derived from the classical Arabic noun *asabiyyah*, roughly translated as a strong group feeling. However, *asabiyyah* is a classical Muslim political term discussed at length by Ibn-e-Khaldun who, in al-Ahsan's words:

> Stated that *'asabiyyah* was a phenomenon which existed within a human being.' Ibn-e-Khaldun never admired this phenomenon; in fact, he explained the word with noticeable unease. But Ibn Khaldun did note that Islamic teachings play an important role in controlling the phenomenon of *'asabiyyah*. (50)

Ta'ssub is the modern Urdu version of the classical *asbiyyah*, which can roughly be translated to the English prejudice. Hali uses it to define a certain kind of prejudicial Muslim attitude within the Indian political framework—their distrust of all things new, and which are not sanctioned by the short-sighted vision of the traditional Muslim mullahs. Thus, coupled with superstition, this becomes another impediment to Muslim progress. Hali explains it as follows:

> Our teachers[14] have taught us thus:
> In every spiritual or worldly undertaking
> Do not follow the example of your opponents
> For this is the real spirit of True Faith
> That you should oppose your opponents' views
> If they say day, you should say night! (81)

This ironic rendition of a particular tradition of the Muslim clergy: opposition for opposition's sake, is one major impediment in the progress of Indian Muslims. This is a particularly important point for Hali, for only from this perspective can he proffer the new modes of education as a remedy for the Muslim nation. This prejudice is not only directed towards other religions alone; Muslim reformers are also a target of it. (Here, of course, Hali is referring to the educational reform efforts of Sayyid Ahmad Khan and the *ulama's* opposition to it). Hali points out: 'If someone wants to introduce reform/You consider him worse than Satan' (83). This brings us to the next major reason for Indian Muslims' downfall: Loss of egalitarianism and lateral solidarity.

As we noted in the discussion on the rise of Islam, one of its causes was the contract between the rich and the poor, that is, that the poor should strive hard and the rich should use their wealth for the public good. Hali considers this a truly Islamic socio-political contract, and considers the failure of this contract as one of the main causes of the fall of Indian Islam. This aspect is expressed by him in the following lines:

> If we had not forgotten the Prophet's teachings:
> That all Muslims are brothers, and
> For as long as a brother aids a brother
> God himself is their protector
> Our ship would have not been destroyed
> And we would have been kings even in our poverty. (84)

This emphasis on lateral solidarity highlights the importance and necessity of such an interaction for the reformation of a nation. What is so brilliant about Hali's thesis is that he is attempting to highlight Muslim weaknesses from a very religious perspective but with clearly secular political goals. If Muslims tried to be less superstitious, less prejudiced, and more closely connected to each other—all attributes of a good Muslim—then the natural process of national regeneration could begin. By streamlining all these aspects of Muslim problems, Hali also opens up a space for Muslim reformers in the name of the same religion that the *ulama* used to castigate any attempts at modern educational reform. After enumerating the other ailments affecting the Muslim community, Hali summarizes the core problems of the Muslims of India in the two concluding stanzas:

> Asked someone of a sage:
> What is the greatest blessing in the world?
> He said: 'Wisdom, for it gives the faith and the world.'
> Asked, What if one does not have wisdom?
> He said: 'Then, knowledge and skill
> For they are the pride of humans.'
> But what if one does not have even these?
> He said: 'Then wealth and materials are best.'
> What if this door is also closed?
> He said: 'Such a man should be struck by lightning.' (106-7)

Here, Hali pinpoints three attributes of a living nation: wisdom, knowledge, and material wealth. The rise of the Muslim civilization, as we have noticed earlier, was caused by a spiritual wisdom that aided the Muslims in having faith, acquiring knowledge and then launching a materially affluent civilization. The order of precedence is also important: wisdom comes first, then knowledge, and then wealth. A nation that possesses none of these attributes might as well be destroyed. Here Hali can speak to the nation and encourage them to 'Forget past delusions/and douse the fires of prejudice' (107), for only then can the Muslim nation of India emerge out of its deep slumber.

From here, Hali takes his readers to the possibilities made available by the British government. Hence, Hali, the national poet of his time, does not perceive the British presence as oppressive, but rather as a progressive change. He writes:

> The government has granted you all freedoms
> The ways of progress are totally open
> It is being heralded all around:
> The king and the people alike are happy
> There is peace all over the lands
> No path is closed to the caravans. (108)

Hali is here quite consistent with the teachings of his mentor and contemporary Sir Sayyid Ahmad Khan who, in the words of one of his biographers, 'was convinced that it was through cooperation with the British alone that Muslims could regain their lost prestige' (Muhammad 222). The tendency to challenge modern education on religious grounds, as Hali challenges here, was a common stance of the majority of the *ulama*. In fact, it had became a part of popular idiom. One good example of it is Badsha Khan's[15] account of a common Pushto chant against modern education:

> *Sabaq de madrase wai para de paise wai*
> *Jannat ke bai zai navi dozakh ke bai ghase wahi*

> Those who learn in schools
> They are none but money's tools
> In heaven they will never dwell,
> They will surely go to hell. (13)

As explained earlier Hali's poem concludes with a summation of the wrongs prevalent in the Muslim society of India; it is in the addendum, included in the second edition, that Hali offers hope for a better future. Here, Hali places all his hopes for positive change through the acquisition of modern knowledge and education. He highlights this as follows:

You have lost the hope of ruling
And have also lost all your wealth
You have also mourned the loss of your courage
And you do not have the wisdom of your elders
Knowledge is all that is left to rely on
For this is the only heritage of the old left. (147)

Having traced the rise of the larger Islamic *ummah* and the specific conditions of the Indian Muslim *qaum*, Hali visualizes a ray of hope only through education. His readers have been told that the glorious past of Islam was due to their quest for knowledge. Hence, the regeneration of the nation now must depend on the same principle of knowledge. By education, he does not mean only religious education; but his ideology of education also encompasses modern, scientific education, the direct cause of European ascendancy. This is that knowledge about which, 'The land and the oceans bear witness/That God's grandeur is contained in knowledge' (148). Hali moves on to the material consequences of knowledge and education, and its inherent linkage with political power. For him, then, modern education is *the* core requirement, not just for the regeneration of the nation, but also for the restoration of lost Muslim prestige and power. Hali combines this quest for knowledge with the need for building an egalitarian lateral Muslim solidarity. Hence, it is through the merging of the former glory of Muslim civilization and acquiring modern education that can reverse the fortunes of Indian Muslims:

Spread the influence of knowledge and skills
So that your progeny attains humanity
So that the poor can attain progress
And the rich are enlightened by its light
Thus will they earn respect in the world
To stabilize the boat of faith and *Millat*. (161)

From this imperative to acquire knowledge, Hali links in his concluding verses of the poem, the need for new knowledge which is imperative for lateral Muslim solidarity. The idea of Muslim political particularity is openly expressed here, that precedes the rise of Indian (Hindu) nationalism. The need for national unity is expressed in the following verses:

Everyone's prestige lies in the prestige of the community
And the community's loss is everyone's loss[16]

Individual prestige or individual rule
Never lasted and shall never last
For only that branch will blossom here
That has its roots planted in the garden. (164)

Hence, Hali has stressed the need for combining Islamic heritage with the imperatives of modernity for the progress of Indian Muslims in his long poem on the rise and fall of Islam. His final message: the Muslims of India must change with the changing times, but for that to happen, they must not forget their glorious heritage, be conscious about their present state of affairs, and chart out a course for the future. Hali, therefore, articulates the idea of nation and its rehabilitation with a combination of memory—universal *ummah*—the present—the Muslim *qaum* of India—and the future through a more nuanced negotiation of British power. And also through mastery of new learning and political awareness. This future can only be realized if the Muslims of India master the new ways of learning and build a larger political community. Hence, what comes across as a religious manifesto, because of the title of the poem, is actually a poem that relies on religious memory but puts its hope in a more secular method of national rehabilitation through the modern system of education. There is, of course, no mention of a Muslim nation-state here, but the poem does solidify the idea of Muslim particularity within the British system. It is this sense of Muslim particularism and exceptionalism that eventually becomes a foundation for the politics of a nation-state. What we also learn here in the process is that the very particularity of Indian Muslims is inherently linked with the Muslim imaginary of *ummah*, and it is this transnational historical link that precludes, at this stage of the Muslim literary production, any territorial articulations of Muslim nationhood. Hence, unlike Bengali Indian nationalism, evident in the works of Bankimcandra Chatterji and others, the Muslim poet, Hali, does not need to retrieve a purist Hindu Vedantic past; that past already forms a larger structure of feeling within which the particularity of Indian Muslims can be articulated.

No discussion of Hali's contribution towards the Muslim consciousness may be complete without throwing some light on his *Muqaddama-e-She'r-o-Shairi* (An Introduction to Poetry). I will focus specifically here on Hali's explanation of the new style of poetry, its chief attributes, and his detailed explication of *nacheral* (natural) poetry. Published in 1893, Hali's *Muqaddama* is probably the most controversial and the most enduring document of Urdu letters. Hali, as stated earlier, was born in Panipat, and therefore, had no entrenched loyalties to either the Lucknow or the Delhi school of poetry, but his staunchest critics belonged to these two schools. In the words of Dr Waheed Qureshi, editor of the *Muqaddama*: 'the publication of the *Muqaddama* caused an uproar. The Lucknow School was furious over the insult to their poets' (19). Unlike Azad, as we will soon find out, Hali's *Muqaddama* was not simply a compilation of the history of Urdu poetry, but he, instead, had challenged its major stylistic and thematic assumptions and introduced a new form in poetry. It was this attempt at changing the shape of Urdu poetry that troubled the followers of older conventions, especially so of the Lucknow school.[17] On the whole, the publication of the *Muqaddama* 'gave a new life to Urdu literature' (Qureshi 20) and forced Urdu poetry to simplify its diction, abandon its dependence on Persian romantic forms, and encouraged poets to write in a more utilitarian vein.[18]

In discussing Hali's *Muqaddama* one important aspect of his main effort must be kept in mind: Hali attempts to free Urdu poetry from the stringent conventional structures of Persianized romantic poetry and to make it into a reformative and didactic tool for the masses. Such poetry must be simple and political. In fact, while emphasizing the political importance of poetry, Hali declares: 'Europeans have always used their ancient poetry for national motivation during hard times' (102). Hali provides us with examples from ancient Greece, Edwardian England, and even discusses the impact of Byron's *Child Harolde* on the Greek struggle against the Turks. He then goes on to narrate the political and historical influence of Arabic poetry, and the role of poets during the tribal wars of the *Jahiliyya* period. These examples of the East and the West are a conscious effort on Hali's part to defend himself from the charge of dwelling exclusively on Western examples, and allows him to suggest that under the current political circumstances, Urdu poetry cannot stay detached and cloistered in its tradition but must become engaged with the popular issues of the Muslims of India. Hali then explains at length the negative influence of 'base poetry' on a society:

> When poetry deteriorates, its poisonous air damages the overall society. When poetry relies on lies and exaggeration, then the nation becomes accustomed to such traits and such poetry becomes acceptable....When strange and supernatural stories enchant the heart, then normal events become less pleasing. False stories become more attractive, and people lose interest in history, geography, mathematics, and science. Hence, slowly and imperceptibly bad habits take root in a society. (*Muqaddama* 122)

Hali's objection to bad poetry is not just based on the aesthetics of the poetry alone: he is more concerned with the affective value of the poetry. Hence, Hali, so insistent upon the public utilitarian role of poetry, must prove first the real-life impact of bad poetry. Here, all ills of the poetry are related to the society and the nation. The general theme that emerges out of this indictment of classical Urdu poetry is simply its non-realistic and exaggerated practice of representing reality. To Hali, both poetry and its audience perpetuate this state of affairs: what poets represent becomes the norm expected by the people, and hence an imperative for the poets to write the kind of poetry that will be admired and appreciated. Base poems may not be badly written; but it is the negative influence that they will have on society which is objectionable. Note also, that for Hali, base poetry takes people away from the study of empirical sciences. As we noticed in the discussion of the *Musaddas*, Hali perceives the acquisition of modern empirical knowledge as a hope for a new Muslim future; hence, any poetry that may discourage the audience from progress and education comes under the category of base poetry. Hence, for Hali, poetry is termed as being base because of the negative influence that it has on society. Thus, conversely, one could argue that for Hali, poetry's role is positive only if it is engaged with the people in an invigorating, progressive dialogue. This takes us to Hali's explanation of *nacheral* poetry. He defines it as follows:

> I deem it important to explain the often-used term *nacheral* poetry. Some people think that it means the kind of poetry associated with *nacheries*,[19] or the poetry that represents the religious ideas of the *nacheries*. Some also think that *nacheral* poetry is the kind of poetry that provides an account of the fall of Muslims or nations. But this is not the case. *Nacheral* poetry means the kind of poetry that corresponds to natural instincts both in its words and its meaning. Words used in *nacheral* poetry must be taken from everyday spoken language; it must be realistic and people should be able to relate to it. (*Muqaddama* 184-5)

This brief explanation of *nacheral* poetry is quite an apt summation of Hali's entire oeuvre. Hali strongly believed in the powerful affective role of poetry in terms of its impact on the nation. By insisting upon a common diction and easily understood meanings, Hali forced Urdu poetry, at least for his followers, out of its romantic detachment and connected it to the people. It can be said that Hali's *Musaddas* was probably the first good example of Hali's brand of poetry, and after Hali finished his long career, both Urdu poetry and prose had become overwhelmingly utilitarian and the writer was inextricably linked with the idea of public good. It is this didactic and reformative function of Urdu literature that I have called political, for after Hali and Azad, the Indian Muslim literature becomes intimately linked with the public, and it is within this linked space that the idea of Muslim particularity is rehearsed, shaped, perpetuated, and finally articulated in nationalistic terms. I will now move on to trace the role of Urdu literature in creating this Muslim particularity with a discussion of the early Urdu novel.

NOTES

1. *Water of Life* is a literal translation of the title. Metaphorically, *Aab-e-Hayat* refers to a mythological hidden spring and drinking the water from which makes one immortal; in the Arab, Persian, and Urdu traditions the immortal guide Khizar (Khid'r in Arabic) is believed to have imbibed from the spring of life and gained immortality. Hence, Azad's title can also be read as a text that immortalises Urdu poetry, while also acting as the spring to give life to the reader.
2. All citations from *Aab-e-Hayaat* are in my translation.
3. *Tazkiras* were the traditional ways of recording events, biographies, and works of poets. Azad is here criticizing the rational model of research that tabulated the minutest details of knowledge. In his views, as the *Tazkiras* were written for a living culture, the writers never felt the need to include minor details like exact dates, dates of publication etc. Hence, Azad's text is also attempting to modernise the writing about the works of his predecessors by including these details as the living culture that obviated the need for such details is no longer there to supplement the written text with an oral discourse. For a good discussion of *Tazkiras* see Francis Pritchett.
4. All citations from Akhtar's work are in my translation.
5. By poem I mean the Urdu *Nazm*, which is closer to the Romantic English poems. The poetical tradition that preceded this era was more focused on the *ghazal*. *Ghazal*, in Azad and Hali's views, was more formalistic and less realistic, and hence not useful for a public function of national reform. These *Mushairahs*, by foregrounding the Urdu *Nazm* become more potent means of public reform. For a detailed discussion of this role of *Nazm* as opposed to *Ghazal* see Francis Pritchett.
6. As I will discuss later, the greatest Muslim poet of India, Muhammad Iqbal, began his career in public *mushairhs* of Lahore.
7. *Musaddas* is a long poem divided into six line stanzas with a rhyme scheme of aa, aa, bb. The complete title of Hali's poem is *Musaddas Maddo Jazr-e-Islam* (The Rise and Fall of Islam)
8. All citations from Hali's *Musaddas* and *Muqaddama* are in my translation.
9. The Urdu word used for the nation is *qaum*, which is derived from the Arabic *qaumiah*. Here, it specifically means the Muslims of India whom Hali sees as one nation, the nation of Islam. Hali's contemporaries also used the term *qaum* to signify Indian Muslims. It is important to note that at this stage of Muslim political consciousness, the term *qaum* is sometimes used interchangeably with the larger concept of *ummah*, the pan-Islamic signifier of Muslim Identity.

10. Here, Hali clearly forestalls the critical responses from the two major schools of Urdu poetry, especially since his poem does not meet the conventional aesthetic standards of both these schools of classical poetry.

11. Traditional religious gatherings arranged on the 12th day of the Muslim month of *Rabi-ul-Awwal* to commemorate the birthday of the Prophet Muhammad [PBUH]. Not all Muslim sects performed this ritual, and it became a contested practice in British India due to the sectarian differences of two major Sunni religious sects. For details on this controversy see Barbara Metcalf.

12. *Huma* is a legendary bird from the Persian poetical tradition. According to the legends, when a land needed a new king, the men stood out in the open to be chosen. *Huma* flew out and the person upon whose head it alighted was declared the king.

13. Instead of giving a verse translation, I am paraphrasing a summation of four of his stanzas. I have considered these as Hali's views about the Hindus because this section of the poem is subtitled 'The Hindu Nations'. Hali uses the same Urdu term—*qaum*—in describing the Hindus.

14. The Urdu word that is used here is *wa'iz*, which literally means someone who teaches through a sermon. Within his peculiar historical time this meant the traditional Muslim mullahs and their sermons in the mosques.

15. Badshah Khan, leader of the Khudai Khitmatgar movement, was a strong ally of Gandhi and opposed the division of India. Though unduly demonised in the departmental history of Pakistan, Badshah Khan's followers now form the most egalitarian, secular political party, the Awami National Party, in the North West Frontier Province of Pakistan. For more details about Badshah Khan's historical role see Sayed Wiqar Ali Shah's work on the subject.

16. This is, of course, a non-literal translation of Hali's verses. The two terms that he uses are *Izz'at* and *Zillat*. The first means respect accorded to or earned by a person or a community; it could also be translated as honour or social capital. *Zillat* is an exact opposite of *Izz'at*, which means the loss of prestige or honour; I have, therefore, translated it as loss.

17. Traditionally the Lucknow School of poetry was more ornate, sensual, and complex; it therefore became an epitome of what Hali considered bad poetry. The Indian poets that Hali chooses as bad examples in the *Muqaddama* are mostly from the Lucknow school, hence the harsh criticism of Hali from Lucknow School critics.

18. For a good discussion of the socio-cultural reasons for Hali's utilitarian stance on Urdu poetry see Francis Pritchett.

19. *Nacheri*, or *Naicari*, was the derogatory term associated with the Muslim reformers, especially Sayyid Ahmad Khan, who attempted to offer naturalistic explanations of Islamic metaphysical phenomenon. For details about Sayyid Ahmad's naturalism, see Aziz Ahmad 40-44.

4

The Early Urdu Novel and Muslim Exceptionalism

The importance of the novel to the modern liberal nation state is a much-rehearsed topic. According to Benedict Anderson, 'it is in the pages of the novel that we see the "national imagination" at work in the movement of a solitary hero through a sociological landscape of a fixity that fuses the world inside the novel with the world outside.' (30) It is in this correspondence between the 'world inside the novel' and the 'world outside' that one may find what Anderson calls 'the technical means for re-presenting the kind of imagined community that is the nation' (25).

The early Urdu novel, however, does not represent the fixity of the nation[1] but the particularity of a Muslim experience in a changed political climate. In its national sense the early Urdu novel traces the negotiation of this altered colonized space by its Muslim hero, and it is in this process that the Muslim particularity and exceptionalism under the raj is articulated. The early Urdu novel is, therefore, both national and supranational in its scope. In as much as it creates an imaginary about negotiating the altered public space, it articulates the particular aspects of Muslim life under the British rule—but in its historical retrieval, by recreating the Muslim empires of the past, it also invokes the supranational concept of the *ummah*. Just as the first English novel, in the words of Ian Watt, becomes emblematic for 'the empire builders' (87), for one can read *Robinson Crusoe's* ventures as a colonial enterprise, the first Urdu novels are didactic and portray the anxieties of individuals at the receiving end of the process of empire-building. As we noticed in the previous chapters, the post-rebellion Muslim literary production slowly changed from its aesthetic emphasis to a utilitarian paradigm. This shift, I have argued, was necessitated by the changed political climate and was aided by the language of loyalism to initiate a new conversation with the British elite, a conversation aimed at creating a space for the Muslims in the British system of power. Hence, the novel's impulse is inherently national, even though it does not invoke the nation-state. Using two of Nazeer Ahmad's novels I will, in this chapter, discuss the role of the novel in articulating a particular Muslim identity, its attempt at creating a hegemonic relationship with the British, and its drive to reconcile the supranational Muslim identity with its particular Indian variant. But my discussion would be incomplete if I did not touch upon an important scholarly debate on the Third World Novel as presented in the pages of *Social Text*: namely, the debate between Fredric Jameson and Aijaz Ahmad. In my opinion, while Jameson tries to read the Third World literary production within its political specificity, Aijaz Ahmad's rebuttal forces the Urdu novel back to the realm of the aesthetics and private sphere. Fredric Jameson's claim of the Third World Novel and the question of national allegory and Aijaz Ahmad's scathing response to Jameson's 'generalizations' can be rehearsed only if the duality of Urdu novel production is effaced. I find both Jameson and Aijaz Ahmad's stances not so mutually exclusive. When read within the context of creating a national mode of thought and exceptionalism, the Muslim Indian novel does turn out to be a national allegory. Here is how Jameson posits his claim about the Third World Novel:

> All third-world texts are necessarily, I want to argue, allegorical, and in a very specific way: they are to be read as what I will call *national allegories,* even when, or perhaps I should say, *particularly* when their forms develop out of the predominantly western machineries of representation, such as the novel. (69)

It is important to note that proving that the Third World Novel is a national allegory is not Jameson's main point; he is attempting to safeguard the reductive readings of the Third World texts by the metropolitan audiences to whom the subjects invoked in the Third World Novel—realist narratives—come as always 'already-read' (Jameson 66). What Jameson means here is that for the metropolitan audiences, the Third World Novel seems to be dated because of its realistic narrative strategies and national setting. As the metropolitan literary production has moved into postmodernism and the age of multinational capitalism, the nationalist novels, for them, tend to seem less mature and atavistic. By attempting to theorize a different mode of reading the Third World Novel, Jameson is also defying the metropolitan impulse to treat history as a universal narrative of progress and replacing it with an idea of multiple histories. Jameson can only posit this claim if he can prove that within the Asiatic Mode of Production, the divide between the political does not sunder the cultural production of the novel and the aesthetic. Hence, in Jameson's words, 'Third-World texts ... necessarily project a political dimension in the form of national allegory: *the story of the private individual destiny is always an allegory of the embattled situation of the public third-world culture and society*' (69). Hence, far from being patronizing, Jameson's attempt here is aimed at introducing a particular technique of reading the Third World texts.

Ahmad's response to Jameson's magisterial attempt at creating a 'cognitive aesthetics' for reading the texts of the periphery is a well-thought-out response to what seems like a gross generalization by Jameson. Aijaz Ahmad is opposed to the idea of positing a blanket-theory of critical reading of the Third World texts simply because of the very diverse nature of the cultural production of the Third World. He challenges Jameson's basic assumptions as follows:

> I shall argue later that since Jameson defines the so-called Third World in terms of its 'experience of colonialism and imperialism,' the political category that necessarily follows from this exclusive emphasis is that of 'the nation,' with nationalism as the peculiarly valorized ideology; and because of this privileging of the nationalist ideology, it is then theoretically posited that 'all Third World texts are necessarily...to be read as...national allegories.' (5-6)

Hence, it seems, Ahmad's main objection happens to be to a blanket description of the Third World reality through the national imaginary, for without that a theory of national allegory of literature would not be possible. This challenge also fractures the binary nature of Jameson's suggestion that the West, somehow, is post national while the rest of the world is still caught in a nationalist paradigm. While constantly challenging Jameson's generalizations about the Third World, Third World Literature, and a unitary method of reading Third World texts, Ahmad finally focuses on the genesis of Urdu literature as an example of the texts that defy Jameson's generalization about 'all Third World texts being the allegory of the nation.' Ahmad, having offered an impressive array of Urdu literary texts, posits his claim in a generalization which is as impressive as that of Jameson:

> I cannot think of a single novel in Urdu between 1946 and 1947, the crucial year leading up to decolonization, which is in any direct or exclusive way about 'the experience of colonialism and imperialism.' In fact, I do not know of *any* fictional narrative in Urdu, in the last roughly two hundred years, which is of

any significance and any length (I am making an exception for a few short stories here), and in which the issue of colonialism or the difficulty of a civilizing encounter between the English and Indian has the same primacy as, for example, in Forster's *A Passage to India* or Paul Scott's *The Raj Quartet*. (21)

This expansive response seems an ideal and convincing challenge to the 'naïve' generalization offered by Jameson, but it is, in itself, a gross generalization. It assumes two points here: it misreads Jameson's claim that all Third-World texts are a response to the colonial experience; and it asserts that despite all the political upheavals of colonial India, the Indian Urdu writers were still content with the realm of the aesthetic and not much concerned with the political. Once again, the culture is privileged over the political to challenge a Western generalization with an equally untenable generalization. Of course, not all Urdu texts were produced with the colonial experience as a backdrop, but colonialism does form a backdrop of many artistic Urdu works in the two hundred years that Ahmad invokes.

In my reading, a shift occurs in the Urdu cultural production after the 1857 rebellion: a shift from what Paul Gilroy calls the 'politics of fulfilment' to the 'politics of trans-configuration' (37). Only, in the Indian context the politics of fulfilment involves the desire for a just and 'non-radicalized' space for Muslims, and eventually a desire for a world—a practical utopia—in which a better Muslim life would be possible. This shift is quite obvious from the first didactic novels of Nazeer Ahmad and becomes more pronounced in the later literary imaginings of the post-partition novels. Hence, the early Urdu novel, instead of being an imaginary literature of the nation-state, mostly dealt with negotiating an altered political landscape within its particular Muslim context. The novel was also a modernized version of the earlier Persianised *Dastaan*, or epic, which was inherently expansive in its scope and supranational in its setting and plot. According to Jawad Ali Zaidi's account, Deputy Nazeer Ahmad was the first Urdu novelist whose first novel *Mirat-ul-Urus* (A Bride's Mirror) was published in 1869. Zaidi also mentions Rattan Nath Sarshar, famous for his long *dastaan Fasana-e-Azad*, and Abdul Haleem Sharar as some other major novelists (248-52), whose major works include *Zawal-e-Baghdaad* (The Decline of Baghdad) and *Firdaus-e-Bareen* (Hidden Paradise). But out of all these novelists, only Nazeer Ahmad's works bear any resemblance to the Western bourgeois novel. *Mirat-ul-Urus* is a didactic novel that portrays a young Muslim woman supporting her husband in succeeding as a civil servant in the British administration. Sarshar's *Fasana-e-Azad* is more of a *Dastaan* and traces the peculiarities of the last days of the native nobility and high culture through the experiences of his protagonist, Azad. Most of Sharar's novels are historical, and hence cover a much larger canvas and focus on supranational themes of the Muslim empire and *ummah*. (The two novels mentioned above deal respectively with the fall of Baghdad to the Mongols, and the tale of Hasan-bin-Sabah's fortress of the assassins in Almut, Iraq). Hence, right from the beginning the Urdu novel was ambivalent about a national consciousness, as the national landscape was under British control, and early novels often dwelt on a nostalgic return to an irretrievable past. Thus, the Urdu novel defies the binary nature of the Jameson–Ahmad debate: it is national and post-national simultaneously.

In my opinion, Nazeer Ahmad is the first Urdu novelist to convert Muslim storytelling from an epic mode to the mode of a realist novel by incorporating two important aspects of the novel, 'time and space' as suggested by Ian Watt (26). Nazeer Ahmad narrates the realistic experiences of his real-life characters across a political landscape governed by the British, and in doing so articulates an imaginative idea of Muslim particularity and exceptionalism within the raj. Nation is used here by me more in context of *qaum* and not nation-state. Hence, the Urdu novel from its very inception was used as a didactic tool for the particularity of the Muslim experience in British India. The novels of Nazeer Ahmad, therefore, focus on the lives of particular individuals and their negotiation of the British power structures. It is important to note here that for Nazeer Ahmad, as well as for later novelists, the two means of inclusion into the British system are either heroic or mundane.[2] Nazeer Ahmad's first novel, *Mirat-ul-Urus*,[3] traces the mundane aspects of material success in the new politico-economic system; while his later novel *Ibn-ul-Waqt* (The Time-Server), traces the impact of an expedited, heroic entry into the British political and cultural realm.

Nazeer Ahmad wrote his first novel to provide a text for the grooming of young girls, hence making the novel—or story-telling—instrumental in training the individual, which itself is the beginning of a path to national consciousness. I will here juxtapose two of Nazeer Ahmad's novels (*Mirat-ul-Urus* and *Ibn-ul-Waqt*) to suggest that the public and private were not necessarily separate and for Nazeer Ahmad, the most important role of the private realm—the *zenana*—was to impact the male negotiation of the public. In his second novel, his concerns are clearly public, and imperialism, the new political order, happens to be the larger structure in which the novel is set and serves as a training ground for the upcoming Muslim elite in negotiating this particular political order.[4] Nazeer Ahmad gives the following reasons for writing his first novel in the preface:

> I had noticed that having seen the men getting their education, the girls had also developed a curiosity about education....Then I looked for a book that would address women's issues in an interesting and non-threatening manner. I looked through the entire book collection and could not find a single such book. It was then that I decided to write this story. (791-2)

The first Urdu novel, it seems, was written because of a strong public imperative: the need to provide an interesting text for the education of women. Before starting his narrative, Nazeer Ahmad also presents his reasons for his support of women's education. As the theme of the novel concerns Muslim women's role in society and education and as his views are posited within the larger domain of traditional Muslim opposition to women's education, the target of the readership is specific to Indian Muslim women. He counters the general objections towards women's education in the following words:

> The hardest thing is that so many consider it odd and sinful to provide education to women. They fear that educated women will become free and might even begin correspondence with unknown men. These are just Satan's whispers and it is unfortunate for this country and for the women. We simply ask: Does education make a person better or worse? If it has adverse effects on character then this should apply to men as well, for their character can also be adversely affected by the same education. (797)

Overall, Nazeer Ahmad builds up his case in the name of the betterment of the nation. As today's young girls will be mothers to future generations, hence their education becomes a national imperative. He also suggests that as 'homemaking cannot be possible without women's help' (799), it is extremely important for women to be educated. With this preamble, the story of two sisters is narrated: one educated; and the other uneducated, and the subsequent impact of their wisdom on their husband's careers and towards the moral well being of their children. Like Hali, he also traces the rise of the British in educational advancement: 'They have come to this country and have governed it so efficiently through the power of knowledge' (804).

Mirat-ul-Urus was first published in 1869. The novel is about the lives of two sisters, Akbari and Asghari, who are diametrically opposed to each other. While Akbari is a typical example of an unwise woman, her sister Asghari epitomizes the successful middle-class woman of her time. It is important to note that unlike Bengali literature, where the native woman was usually juxtaposed with her westernized other, in *Mirat-ul-Urus*, the comparison is based on knowledge of native customs and culture, and the one possessed with native wisdom and who realizes the changes occurring outside the domain of the *zenana* is posited as a successful woman. Hence, the novel is not simply about the private sphere, but rather, about the impact that wisdom in the private sphere has on male success in the public realm. In my brief discussion of the novel, my focus will be on Asghari, the educated sister.

Unlike her elder sister, Akbari, Asghari is a model of foresight and prudence. She begins her married life as a child bride of thirteen while her husband is still in school. The first major change that she brings into the life of her husband is to encourage him to attain a more useful education like 'arithmetic and language of the courts to find a job' (886). Her husband, Muhammad Kamil, upon her advice, begins to learn Arabic and arithmetic more seriously, and while he is busy with his studies, Asghari begins to run a neighbourhood school for girls which is quite successful. Finally they reach a point where Asghari encourages her husband to find a job. While discussing Kamil's job prospects, Asghari rejects her husband's suggestion to seek Asghari's father's assistance in aiding him to find a job in the government. Asghari opines:

> Since English administration began, the native nobility has deteriorated; so you should look for employment with the English (912).

When Kamil informs her of the impossibility of getting employment with the English, Asghari suggests the following:

> I know that thousands are looking for these jobs, but those who do have them are people just like you...you must develop a rapport with those who are already working in these jobs; since from them you will learn of any available vacancies and you might reach some administrator through them. (912)

These lines show that the wife who traditionally was considered as the custodian of the private areas of life, is well-informed about the public realm. What Asghari is conveying here is the significance of contacts. Not only does she know which jobs are better (English over the natives), but she is also able to provide her husband with a means to achieve this goal. It is in this negotiation of the public domain by the wife—the traditional inhabitant of the private domain, that the novel becomes political. A successful wife is not only one who is well-versed in household affairs, but also, remaining within the confines of tradition, is able to provide sound advice beyond the home, the man's world. Hence, the national role of women is introduced here, which is an expansion beyond the confines of their historical role of safeguarding the traditions. It now includes their role in playing a part in their husband's (inhabitants of the public domain) public life, by urging them to learn to negotiate the changed political order and the altered job market. There are traditional and modern sources for the introduction of this particular role of women. In a major work written specifically for women, Maulana Ashraf Ali Thanewi emphasized this rational role of women. He was of the opinion that a virtuous woman can be a positive influence in her husband's life; and a foolish woman negative. In his famous and most widely distributed work *Beheshti Zewar* (Heavenly Ornaments) he stresses the importance of his views as follows:[5]

> For quite some time I witnessed the religious deterioration in Muslim women and thought of offering a remedy. My main worry was that this deterioration was not only limited to their religious aspect, but could also impact their worldly lives including the lives of their children and husbands. Knowing that women's ignorance of religious knowledge can impact the future of their children as well as the world around them, I searched for any books in Urdu that may be of educative value for women. It was decided that one such book should be compiled exclusively for women that should, in simple language, explain all matters of religion pertaining to women. (6-8)

Another Muslim reformer, Mumtaz Ali,[6] had a different approach towards the issue. He, as explained by Aziz Ahmad, believed in complete equality between men and women (72). Nazeer Ahmad's views on women's education were traditional and he, unlike Mumtaz Ali, was adamant over the importance of *purdah* for women. In fact, despite his obvious Anglophilia, he declares in one of his letters to his son:

> The entire edifice of our [social] character depends upon the *purdah*. The day women lose this emphasis on *purdah*, the entire building will collapse (Nazeer Ahmad *Mu'za* 216).

The novel concludes with Kamil becoming a successful civil servant of British India due to the sound advice provided to him by Asghari. David Lelyveld includes a comprehensive discussion of Kamil's upward mobility within what he calls the 'Kachari Milieu' (64) in his analysis of the novel. By *Kachari* (court) Milieu, Lelyveld means the role of the court system in creating a new form of *sharif* (noble) culture where 'people with no prior connection to each other' (64) could meet and exchange views. But I am looking at the novel from a slightly different angle, and in my opinion, what the first Urdu novel teaches us is that the main concern of the novel—the most nationalistic of the literary genres—was the possibility of Muslim upward mobility within the British system of rewards. This breaking-in into the British system of governance, as I pointed out earlier, follows a mundane process. What is instructive about the novel is its emphasis on the role of women in making this public negotiation of the British power possible, and the linkage of the importance of women's role with the public domain. The novel imparts a positive form of womanhood. The two terms that Nazeer Ahmad uses to describe his two main female characters are *sughar* (competent, industrious) and *phuhar* (incompetent, unimaginative). A *sughar* daughter or wife is considered a blessing. She can alter the fortune of the entire family through her wisdom, patience, and foresight; whereas a *phuhar* wife or daughter could ruin all. In such cultural imagination of the role of women in the success of a family, the public success of men is inextricably linked with the women in their lives. Nazeer Ahmad's Asghari is a new kind of *sughar* woman, for she now must have wisdom enough to ensure her husband's success in a changed public sphere. Since the novel is specifically written for Muslim women and as it traces a Muslim's success within the British public domain, the novel, therefore, articulates the very Muslim particularity which includes: a Muslim novelist; Muslim characters; and a Muslim audience. It is this articulation of a specifically Muslim experience in the pages of the novel that makes it a novel of Muslim national consciousness. To discuss the political implications of the Muslim–British relationship, I will now move on to discuss *Ibn-ul-Waqt*, in detail.

Considering *Ibn-ul-Waqt* a representative novel of Nazeer Ahmad, Saleem Akhtar, the editor of *Majmua* (Collected Works of Nazeer Ahmad), suggests the following about its immediate context:

> Nazeer Ahmad finished this novel in 1888. By then the Rebellion had ended and the English government had become an irrefutable reality. The defeat had wiped the Muslim minds of any delusions of power and government and the deeds of the Mughal Empire had become the tall tales of *Arabian Nights*. The Muslims were left only with a few customs and traditions that they considered instrumental in saving their national pride....It is within this context that

Nazeer Ahmad matured as a literary figure, and hence he was champion of utilitarian[7] literature. (36)

Set in Delhi immediately after the rebellion, *Ibn-ul-Waqt* deals with the consequences of a heroic entry into the British system. But first, a few words about the title, which is also the name of the novel's main character. In Urdu and Persian *Ibn-ul-Waqt* literally means 'the son of time'. Used always as a derogatory term, it implies a person whose views alter with the changing circumstances. The editor also informs us that Nazeer Ahmad's characters are invariably always based on character types and their names represent their type (37). Hence, the novel, through the struggles of its main character, traces the struggles of a certain type but this representation does seem to possess a degree of particularity to make him a real-life character.

Ibn-ul-Waqt is Nazeer Ahmad's most overtly political novel and it openly deals with the post-rebellion Muslim dilemma of negotiating the British ascendancy. Within this struggle, Nazeer Ahmad also highlights the problems faced by Muslim reformers in this struggle including the limits of native assimilation and popular Muslim perception of westernisation. It is in this complex view of the British system by a native that a more overt representation of post-rebellion Muslim particularity finds its most coherent and cogent expression. The novel starts with the following declaration:

> Nobody would have noticed it during our time, but the reason Ibn-ul-Waqt got so much notoriety was because he adopted the English ways at a time when learning English was considered *kuf'r*, and when using English things was similar to *irtadad*. (51)

This first sentence captures two very important aspects of the post-rebellion Muslim condition; it implies that the current views of the Muslims are different, and the story is about a time when Muslims looked negatively upon the British and their system. Being a British civil servant himself, this clarification of the narrative time ensures that Nazeer Ahmad's work could not be construed as a critique of the current British policies, while still giving him the freedom to look at the immediate past—of Muslim–British relations—with a more critical insight. The last part of the sentence is also instructive, for it gives us a representation of Muslim views of the British in the past; the Muslims of the narrative time of the novel saw an interaction with the British within the general rubric of two cardinal sins: *kuf'r* and *irtadad*. *Kuf'r* signifies the world outside Islam; all those, except the people of the book, are in a state of *kuf'r*, or non-belief. Hence, during the narrative time of the novel, the British system and any association with it was, in popular imagination, equal to being in contact with *kuf'r*. *Irtadad*, meaning apostasy, signifies the impact of dealing with the British or using British products or materials: one feared the loss of one's religion. Hence, Nazeer Ahmad informs us that the hero, Ibn-ul-Waqt, lived in such times. This is probably the reason why his story became a public scandal.[8] This novel is of particular importance since it highlights an incipient narrative of Muslim exceptionalism immediately after the Rebellion.

The novel is set in Delhi and the narrative starts while the rebellion is already in progress. The rebellion provides Ibn-ul-Waqt, a member of a noble family working for the Mughal court, a chance of a heroic entry into the British world. When he is on his way home from the mosque, Ibn-ul-Waqt is intercepted by a stranger who addresses him: 'My name is Jan Nisar; I am one of the Pathans of Bhadurpur' (58). Jan Nisar further informs Ibn-ul-Waqt that he works for a gentleman [English] Magistrate Mr Noble, who has been shot by the rebels, and pleads with Ibn-ul-Waqt to rescue his injured master. What is instructive here is the word *talangas* by which Jan Nisar describes the rebels. *Talangas* is a slang word in Urdu for riff-raff or the mob.[9] Hence, just as we saw in Ghalib's representation of the rebels, here too, no sympathy is portrayed by Nazeer Ahmad for the rebels. This could be attributed to two factors: class difference between the rebels and Nazeer Ahmad; and the fact that Nazeer Ahmad's main emphasis is to create a pro-British public consciousness. Hence, at this stage of Muslim literary production, it is imperative for writers to highlight Muslim loyalty to the British and to present the Rebellion as an anomaly. Ibn-ul-Waqt agrees to help Jan Nisar's master and his reply, once again, exemplifies the kind of view Nazeer Ahmad and his cohorts want to present of the rebellion: 'Whatever these sinners and *namakharaam talangas* are doing is certainly wrong; it is not permitted in any religion. I consider it my human duty to save your *sahib*. (59)

This altruistic act of compassion grants Ibn-ul-Waqt instant access to the British power structure as soon as British rule is restored. He rescues Mr Noble and nurses him to health certainly under extremely dangerous conditions. This post-rebellion mode of altruistic heroism is certainly based on reality: Sir Sayyid was one such native responsible for saving the lives of two English ladies. What is important about its rendition in fiction is that it provides us with a vision of the British expectation of the natives during the rebellion. Even though the East India Company had not done much to create a hegemonic relationship with the natives, in the post-rebellion world, the only way for the Muslims to prove their loyalty was to convince the British beyond doubt that they had aided them during the time of the rebellion. Hence, with very limited means and mundane methods of mobility available, the Muslims breaking-in into the British system, especially in the immediate aftermath of the rebellion, was by and large based on such heroic measures.

As a reward for his coming to the aid of a local magistrate, Ibn-ul-Waqt finds himself showered by British attention after the rebellion. Nazeer Ahmad describes his induction into the British power-sphere:

> During the Durbar [a formal ceremony] Ibn-ul-Waqt was number 125 amongst the well-wishers of the British government. When he shook the Commissioner's hand, he was given the title to the confiscated land of the Sikh rebel, the *zamindaar* of district Gor Ganoh; it was a claim of three thousand rupees/year granted to him as an inheritable estate. While he received his award, Mr Noble nodded his congratulations to him from behind the Commissioner. (77)

Suddenly, Ibn-ul-Waqt, who until then had been a devout Muslim and lived with his extended family, finds himself at the centre of attention of the new dominant power in Delhi, and the reward precipitates his transition into British circles. He eventually buys a house in the city and adopts British ways: 'Living alone in a large secluded house with house servants, wearing English attire, keeping dogs,[10] and entertaining British officials.[11] All these aspects of urban life were considered strictly European, especially the practice of keeping dogs inside the home, and could be culturally read as *irtadad* (apostasy). Now this move into the British system and especially adopting British ways cannot be sustained unless rationalized through its linkage to the public good: the public imperative. Ibn-ul-Waqt, therefore, on Mr Noble's insistence, decides to become a reformer. During his first meeting with the Englishman, Ibn-ul-Waqt holds a lengthy discussion with the former; the focus of the discussion is the rebellion, its causes, and the role of Muslims in it. It is during this discussion that Mr Noble shares his views of the post-rebellion period with Ibn-ul-Waqt:

> We must understand that even before the Rebellion the Muslims, except for about a dozen families, were in a bad shape. This Rebellion has made their condition even worse. I don't think anyone has come out unscathed from it.

Now the problem of the cartridge[12] had first mobilized the Hindus but the blame has completely been laid on the Muslims. These foolish Muslims, out of national affiliation, supported the Hindus and brought so much harm to themselves that it would take years for them to rise again. (100-101)

This passage, through the words of a British official, represents the two main concerns of the Muslim elite as well as the people: Muslim poverty, both before and after the rebellion and the role of the Hindus in it. The entire passage, of course, is an attempt at rehabilitating the Muslims by shifting the blame of the rebellion onto the Hindus. Even more important for my inquiry is this emphasis on the degree of Muslim particularity: the Hindu-Muslim differences did not suddenly flare-up at the time of the nationalist movement. Here, in one of the early works of Muslim fiction, the Muslims are already expected to make their case with reference to the Hindus. The Muslim struggle, therefore, is not necessarily against the British, but must be juxtaposed with their stronger and more successful counterparts, the Hindus.

In this particular meeting, Mr Noble encourages Ibn-ul-Waqt to become a reformer, and according to him a reformer 'does something that benefits the whole nation and the one that is called a prophet [Prophet Muhammad (PBUH)] was also a reformer' (103). These are comforting words for Ibn-ul-Waqt, for, since he has already adopted British ways, being a reformer, then, grants him the means to legitimize his affiliation with the new political Order. This discussion between the two characters also highlights the absolute need for reform by the Muslims of India. It is, however, important to note that the reform here is not religious but secular in nature. Noble informs Ibn-ul-Waqt that 'the greatness of Europe does not lie in its political power; but rather in the power of its knowledge' (105), and the Muslims of India may reach such heights by acquiring Western knowledge. This stress upon the acquisition of Western knowledge is quite the same as what Altaf Hussain Hali presented in his poem discussed in the preceding chapter. Towards the end of their discussion, Ibn-ul-Waqt is converted to Noble's point of view and decides to become a Muslim reformer. Another important aspect of their discussion must be kept in mind here: it is the Muslims who are in need of this reform; hence Ibn-ul-Waqt, as a Muslim, must bear the responsibility of leading his people as a reformer. This particularity of the novel must be kept in mind: it is a novel written by a Muslim author with Muslim characters, one of whom decides to become a reformer, for the conditions of the Muslims, we are told, are much worse than their Hindu counterparts. We must read this particularity of the novel as an example of Muslim exceptionalism within the realm of British Indian politics. It is also important to note that the text does not generate this exceptionalism. The public imperative within the novel—the Muslim conditions and Ibn-ul-Waqt's need for legitimation—inscribe this need to help the fellow Muslims in the novel.

Another important aspect of the novel is its comparative value with one of its Bengali Hindu counterparts: Bankimcanra Chatterji's *Anadamath*. Published in 1882, the reason the latter seems so nationalist a work is because it matches our critical expectations of an anticolonial novel: the novel focuses on the Sanyasi rebellion that followed the famine of 1770 and describes the early nationalism of Bengali Hindus within a Muslim Bengal including the defeat of the East India Company troops. Bankim's novel, however, despite the contrary assertions of Julius Lipner,[13] the translator, successfully introduces the idea of a militant Bengali Hindu subject in conflict with its Muslim counterpart.

Nazeer Ahmad's project, however, is much different: he and his contemporary Muslim elite are attempting to create a space for the Muslims within the British system. His work, therefore, must posit itself in the language of loyalty to the British and in opposition to the Hindus but not necessarily in terms of war, for the project is, precisely, to transform the war-like Muslims into loyal subjects of the Crown. It is this project that in itself should be read as a particular form of Muslim nationalistic literature.

Because of its emphasis on creating a space for the Muslims within the British system of rewards, Ibn-ul-Waqt insists on transforming the Muslim–English relationship from that of dominance to hegemony. The importance of hegemony is undeniable for the post-rebellion Muslims of India, and it is in this need of a hegemonic relationship where my discussion of British politics differs from that of Ranjit Guha. Using Ibn-ul-Waqt as a representative Muslim text, I will now briefly respond to Guha's main argument in one of his major works about British rule in India.

In his essay, 'Dominance Without Hegemony and its Historiography', Ranjit Guha portrays the following picture of the indigenous bourgeoisie:

> Pliant and prone to compromise from their inception, they lived in a state of happy accommodation with imperialism for the greater part of their career as a constituted political force between 1885 and 1947. The destruction of the

colonial state was never their project. They abjured and indeed resolutely
opposed all forms of armed struggle against the raj, and settled for pressure-
politics as their main tactical means in bargaining for power. (213)

Guha further suggests that the order established by the British was
primarily based on dominance and was never really hegemonic. This
process of dominant hegemony, he suggests, was derived 'from two
distinct paradigms, one of which is typically British and the other Indian'
(233). These two paradigms are the British idiom of Order and the Indian
idiom of *Danda* (237). By idiom of *Danda*, Guha implies: 'All the semi-
feudal practices and theories of power which had come down intact from
the pre-colonial era or were remoulded...under the impact of colonialism'
(238). These two idioms of dominance—Order and *Danda*—Guha
suggests, combined to form an idiom of Obedience that launched and
sustained the native bourgeoisie's 'loyalist discourse' (254). According to
Guha's further discussion, the idiom of Obedience informed 'the many
shades of compromise between collaboration and dissent which were so
characteristic of elite nationalism' (256). What is written out of the
colonial equation, in Guha's assertion, is the possibility of rebellion and
insurrection. This reliance on two paradigms eventually causes the failure
of the universalist drive of capital that Guha describes as follows:

> The answer simply is that colonialism could continue as a relation of power
> in the subcontinent *only on the condition* that the colonizing bourgeoisie should
> fail to live up to its own universalist project... In other words, D *[dominance]*
> *as a term of the central relation of power in the subcontinent meant Dominance*
> *without hegemony.* (274-275)

This answer becomes clearer if Guha's question is kept in sight: 'How is
it that even at its hour of triumph the universalist tendency was resigned
to live at peace with the heterogeneity and particularity of political culture
of an Asian colony?' (274). What Guha means by, 'capital's universalist
drive,' is its capacity to eliminate 'what was parochial and particularistic
in metropolitan politics.' (273). Guha reads the failure of the universalizing
impact of capital as a failure of its hegemonic project. There is an
important point of disagreement between my analysis and that of Guha's.
It is in the manner in which he has defined the colonizer's 'universalist
project'. What Guha seems to suggest is that since the colonizing project
could not replicate the universalizing effect that it had accomplished
within the metropolitan cultures, it therefore never culminated in
hegemony. I think the creation of British hegemony in India was

contingent upon a non-universalist paradigm, which, in order to create a hegemonic relationship, focused more on the particularities of the native groups. Had it been universalist in nature—which many Anglicans desired it to be—it would have then become a relationship of dominance aimed at altering and homogenizing Indian culture through force. The construction of British hegemony depended upon the failure of its universalist drive in accommodating native differences. It is this aspect of the hegemony that the Muslim elite in the post-rebellion world attempted to highlight. In this process, then, the elite trade-off the popular interest in order to obtain material advantages from the British. This aspect of the Anglo–Muslim relationship is important for my inquiry. The Muslim elite, as I have suggested earlier, having witnessed the post-rebellion deteriorating conditions of Muslims, must therefore, attempt to negotiate a new contract with the British. This new contract must ensure special political and economic advantages for the Muslims in exchange for their loyalty to their British rulers. This loyalty, of course, must be won by the British through a system of rewards, which makes it imperative on the part of the British to create a hegemonic relationship with the Muslims. Hence, they must write the rebellion out of the immediate history and replace it with a promise of loyalty. Their approach to the British power is, therefore, not a capitulation but a complex web of the politics of survival. The Muslim elite must, therefore, write the rebellion out of their history, or at least push it to the edge, and foreground their loyalty in order for Muslims to be included in the British system of power.

It is in this process that Ibn-ul-Waqt's role as a reformer becomes extremely significant. He must serve as a liaison between his people and the British rulers, and acquaint the latter about the plight of his Muslim brethren; at the same time emphasizing upon his people of the material and other benefits that they would receive in return for their loyalty towards the British. At the post-dinner speech that he gives at his initiation ceremony, Ibn-ul-Waqt highlights the dichotomy existing between British expectations and their pre-Rebellion policies:

> The British conquered this country by the sword and put down the Rebellion by the sword as well. But they cannot control the bodies and hearts of the people by the sword. For centuries the people of this country have been subjects of despots, and until now they have not really seen the real face of the British Empire. It is, therefore, imperative on the British officials that besides performing their duties, they should also present themselves as the representatives of the Queen....The British treat the natives with such contempt that no one wishes to interact with them unless it is absolutely

necessary. To create love and respect between the two is like expecting a lion and a goat to be together...The British complaint after the Rebellion is that the Hindustanis did not come to their aid, but they should first question themselves: What favours and deeds of kindness have they displayed to *earn* such support from the Hindustanis? (Emphasis added 126-127)

Ibn-ul-Waqt here is clearly broaching the subject of hegemony. His criticism of the British is couched in his reference to the real British Order—personified in the Queen—and the non-British behaviour of the British officials. According to this view, for as long as the relationship is based on dominance alone, there can be no expectations of loyalty; the British have simply not *earned* this loyalty. Hence, in order for them to obtain the willing help of the natives, a relationship of love and kindness must be established. In other words, the establishment of a hegemonic relationship. Hence, the language of loyalty and idiom of Obedience, for the Muslims at this stage, is not a failure of the bourgeois promise but a necessity. Ibn-ul-Waqt's speech, therefore, is a good example of this contract between the native Muslims and the British. The British must earn the native Muslim sympathy through kindness and love: they must transform a relationship of dominance to hegemony. As the Muslims had just recently participated in a rebellion and were suffering its consequences, the language of loyalty is the only way in which they can be included within the British order. It is in this particular situation that the language of Muslim nationhood takes a loyalist turn and becomes a constant trope in the later constitutional politics of the All-India Muslim League. Ibn-ul-Waqt's suggestion, therefore, is the very cornerstone of Muslim politics of survival as seen by the loyalist elite.

Loyalism certainly was not the only approach towards Muslim–British relations. Nazeer Ahmad, through his novel, also makes the reader aware of the two extremes of Muslim politics prevailing at the time: the politics of the *ulama*, and the politics of the loyalists. These two competing views of the Indian Muslims are presented in the form of a dialogue between Ibn-ul-Waqt and his bother-in-law, Hujjat-ul-Islam. While Ibn-ul-Waqt represents the loyalist school, Hujjat-ul-Islam (the voice of Islam) represents the non-assimilative views of the *ulama*. Nazeer Ahmad describes the second impediment in the way of the loyalists: Muslim distrust of the British, and their westernized ways. While Ibn-ul-Waqt succeeds in carving out a place for himself within the British Order; it seems that his unbalanced adoption of British values makes him a suspect in the eyes of his own community, hence making his vision of reform an impossible task. As stated earlier, the reformer must go through a dual process of negotiation, i.e., adopting British ways, but at the same time, retaining a certain degree of Muslim cultural specificity. It is this dilemma of the loyalist elite that Hujjat-ul-Islam highlights in his dialogue with Ibn-ul-Waqt. Nazeer Ahmad introduces Hujjat-ul-Islam as a foil to Ibn-ul-Waqt:

> Hujjat-ul-Islam had left for Hajj before the Rebellion of 1857. He only heard the rumours of it in Arabia. He reached Bombay about twenty days after the fall of Delhi. He could have come back to Delhi earlier, but as the Muslims were being persecuted in Delhi, he decided to go to Calcutta by sea and then enter his hometown from Madras...He was informed of Ibn-ul-Waqt's change of ways and his aunt had requested him to visit them to help. (194)

Hujjat-ul-Islam is summoned by the ladies of Ibn-ul-Waqt's household to salvage them from the public embarrassment caused by the latter's changed ways. Meanwhile, Ibn-ul-Waqt's fortunes have taken a bad turn: he has lost it all and is in trouble with his superiors on trumped up corruption charges. It is in the midst of these circumstances that Hujjat-ul-Islam returns to Delhi. When he reaches Ibn-ul-Waqt's Western bungalow, the first thing he notices is that there is no mosque close by; and no proper area in the house to offer one's prayers since, 'each room is adorned with pictures' (199). It is obvious that Ibn-ul-Waqt has completely abandoned the Islamic obligation of daily prayer. These impressions of Hujjat-ul-Islam of his cousin's changed status are a backdrop of his later discussions with Ibn-ul-Waqt. It may also be termed as the clash of Hujjat-ul-Islam's metaphysical beliefs and Ibn-ul-Waqt's rationalist emphasis. Their discussion over the limits of human will manifests their opposing philosophical views of life:

> **Ibn-ul-Waqt:** Our differences are mostly semantic. You accept that humans have limited will and so do I....But what I am suggesting is that if man continues progressing at the same pace as the last few hundred years, he will one day become master of his own health and his own life.

> **Hujjat-ul-Islam:** May God forgive you for such beliefs. Do you actually believe that man would, some day, God forbid, become God?

This brief discussion is a good example of the naturalist tendencies of the loyalist school (the *nacheries*) headed by Sayyid Ahmad Khan, a group Nazeer Ahmad was sympathetic to, and the *ulama* who were sceptical of the natural explanations of religion. What is important to note here is that any such natural and rationalist explanations of life could be construed as un-Islamic, and thus by extension, an adoption of British values and modes of thought in itself became suspect. Both these characters engage in several discussions of this type in which two extremely opposite views of life are juxtaposed. In the end, Hujjat-ul-Islam leaves Ibn-ul-Waqt with the following parting message:

> You are trying to reach the world of God in your first flight; when in fact, you should first solve the riddle of this world. If you are really interested in faith then adopt the following straight approach: the existence of this world and its order suggests that there is a creator...Though we cannot see God, nor can we discover all his attributes through intellect; his creations bear witness to his existence. This is true faith. The religion has two parts: first, you must inhabit an Islamic self and then choose a sect of Islam that you like. If you do this, and when Islam's true beauty finds its place in your mind then you will find this English mode of life quite oppressive. (170-171).

The book *Ibn-ul-Waqt* concludes with these lines. The task of the Muslim loyalist reformer is further complicated by the traditional point of view. The reformer, in order to be effective must also be a pious Muslim. The novel, thus, foregrounds the importance of double negotiation: the Muslim elite will only be able to lead the Muslim masses if they do not lose their sense of self and Muslim identity in the process of dealing with the British. It was this important aspect of the native Muslim identity that forced the British to abandon their universalist project and change their policies specific to the perceptions of the natives. Respecting local religions and maintaining Muslim family law, thus, were a means of creating a hegemonic relationship. On the other hand, if the British had implemented their own cultural values—as the Anglicists insisted—then the raj would have remained a system of dominance. In case of Muslims, this insistence on maintaining a Muslim identity defines the *ulama*'s response to the loyalists. I will, in the next chapter, discuss the major dissenting voices from the traditionalists who were opposed to Nazeer Ahmad and Sayyid Ahmad Khan's loyalist tendencies.

NOTES

1. Here Sara Suleri's criticism of Anderson's approach to cultural nationalism is quite apt. For details see Suleri 7-10.

2. By heroic I mean an action, usually altruistic, that causes instant approval by the British and causes an immediate entry into the power system. The most oft repeated heroic action in post-rebellion fiction and reality were the attempts by the natives to save a British official or any of their dependents during the rebellion. This heroic deed becomes a constant trope in Muslim fiction, especially in terms of explaining someone's sudden rise within the post-rebellion political system. In real life, Sayyid Ahmad Khan's actions to save two British ladies became the strongest proof of his loyalty to the British in the post-rebellion period. Surprisingly, even the postcolonial Urdu writers use this trope in tracing the rise of certain Indian Muslim families in post-rebellion India, one good example of which is Abdullah Hussain's *The Weary Generations*. What I have called the mundane method of vertical mobility is also made possible through loyalty but is dependent mostly on acquisition of education.

3. All citations from Nazeer Ahmad's works are in my translation.

4. It is important to note that the Urdu novel is both national and post-national in its scope. I am here explaining its nationalistic production, while I will explain the post-national aspects of the novel at a later stage.

5. My translation. This citation is a summation of the author's ideas.

6. Mumtaz Ali was a contemporary of Nazeer Ahmad and famous for his work *Haquq-e-Niswan* (The Rights of Women). According to Aziz Ahmad, Mumtaz Ali reinterpreted the Qur'anic verses about women's rights and suggested a radical new approach to the rights of women, including abolition of the *purdah* system. For details see Aziz Ahmad 72-76.

7. Saleem Akhtar uses the Urdu word *Maqsadiat*, which literally means something with an aim. I have translated it as utilitarian because it is the utility of literature as a tool for public betterment that is meant by the Urdu term.

8. According to Aziz Ahmad, the main character also caricatures people like Sir Sayyid Ahmad Khan who had adopted a 'bicultural' way of life. For details see Aziz Ahmad 36.

9. It is also important to note that the term *talanga* was also used to refer to the native soldiers enlisted in the army of the East India Company, especially those who wore a British uniform.

10. In most Islamic cultures, dogs are considered unclean and are not permitted in the inner sanctum of the house. Keeping dogs as household pets, therefore, was seen as an obvious example of Westernisation.

11. During the narrative time of the novel, eating together with the foreigners was also considered un-Islamic in popular imagination, which was probably a strong Hindu influence on Indian Islam. Nazeer Ahmad and Sayyid Ahmad Khan tried to dispel this prejudice by arguing that as the British were people of the book, breaking bread with them could not be considered a contaminating experience. Sayyid Ahmad also asserted that this practice of not sharing food with non-Muslims was strictly un-Islamic and was caused by Hinduization of Indian Islam.

12. It is believed that one of the main reasons for the early mutiny of the Indian soldiers was due to a new kind of ammunition. The soldiers had to bite off a part of the cartridge before inserting it into their muskets. A rumour suggested that the cartridge contained cow and pig fat in it; hence making it religiously offensive to both Hindus and Muslims. Here Noble is referring to the same incident.

13. For details of Lipner's discussion of the Hindu–Muslim aspects of the novel see Julius Lipner 67-124.

5

The Critique of Loyalism and the Neo-Traditionalists: Shibli Naumani and Akbar Allahabadi

As mentioned earlier, Sayyid Ahmad Khan's loyalist group was not the only group competing for the hearts and minds of the Muslims of India; even Nazeer Ahmad, as becomes obvious at the end of his novel, had his differences with the complete adoption of British values. The other extreme in Muslim politics were the *ulama* whose view of the British was based on a purist Muslim identity. In the middle of these two extremes were the writers and scholars who occupied an ambivalent position. They could be described, as in Anthony D. Smith's words, as the neo-traditionalists. Smith provides us with the following definition of neo-traditionalism:

> The first route, that of neo-traditionalism, tries to accept the technical achievements and some of the methods of western science and rationalism without any of its underlying assumptions. Socially and politically, it utilizes modern methods of mobilizing people but for traditionalist ends. ('The Crisis' 117).

Within the Indian Muslim context, the neo-traditionalists had strong pan-Islamic tendencies and produced literature more critical of the English as well as the loyalists. Their position, however, was not irreconcilably opposed to each other but differed in its approach to the question of Muslim revival. They, however, shared their views on the question of Muslim exceptionalism, and despite their differences with the reformers, did reinforce Muslim particularity through their works. In this chapter I will briefly discuss the literary works of two major neo-traditionalists: Maulana Shibli Naumani[1] and Akbar Allahabadi. I have chosen these two literary figures for the importance of their work but also because they both make it a point to criticize the loyalist policies of Sayyid Ahmad Khan, Altaf Hussain Hali and others, while still not outrightly opposed to maintaining close contact with the British. Also, the emphasis on Muslim tradition makes their work comparative to the trans-historical and trans-national Muslim context. Hence, by connecting their literary production to colonial excesses against the Muslims all over the world, the neo-traditionalists are able to articulate a different kind of native subjectivity: that of a questioning subject. This critical and questioning subject had existed in the works of the *ulama* all along, but had articulated its criticism of the colonizers only within the religious arena. The neo-traditionalists, because of their ambivalent space between the two extremes, were able to popularize this particular subjectivity and make it an important voice of native Muslim literature. My discussion of the works of Shibli Naumani and Akbar Allahabadi will further explain this important aspect of the neo-traditionalist literary production.

Shibli Naumani worked closely with Sayyid Ahmad Khan. He was the Head of the Department of Theological Studies at the Muhammadan Anglo Oriental (MAO) College, that was set up by Sir Sayyid. Aziz Ahmad provides the following introductory account of Shibli Naumani:

> Steeped in conservative classical Muslim scholarship, his mind was also open to the challenges and inspirations of western orientalists. Unlike Sayyid Ahmad Khan, he was more sensitive to the pull of pan-Islamism....He created the tradition of Islamic historiography in Urdu; but he also gave it a strong conservative colour of revivalism. The methodology he developed was a synthesis of the traditional Islamic disciplines of chronicles and hagiography and the western discipline of objective analysis. (77)

With Shibli Naumani, then, Muslim literature is geared towards the Islamic past and its pan-Islamic present to define the particularities of the Muslims of India. In his popular works he insists upon the need to retrieve the stories of past Muslim heroes. He was, therefore, not necessarily opposed to Western education and viewed Sayyid Ahmad Khan's reformatory efforts in a positive light; but at the same time he did not want the Muslim youth to lose touch with their history. He stresses upon the importance of this aspect in one of his essays:[2]

> Someone has aptly pointed out that our misfortune is not only that we have been conquered by the Europeans; but they have also succeeded in conquering our dead. When we speak of courage, strength, honour and knowledge, it is the European heroes we talk of...not our own. The reason for this does not

lie in the fact that we no longer revere our own heroes, but because modern
education does not provide us with an opportunity to learn the accomplishments
of our ancestors. (Naumani 4)

Hence, it becomes Naumani's mission to recover and translate as much
of Muslim history as possible, including the beginning of a project to
write a comprehensive *Sira* (biography) of the prophet, parts of which he
had finished before his death in 1914 and which was published
posthumously by one of his students, Sayyid Suleman Nadwi. One of the
main aims of Naumani's *Sira* was to respond to the distortions present in
the Western historiography about the life of the Prophet Muhammad
(PBUH). That is why he includes a fairly extensive introductory chapter
on the European publications on the Prophet's life, and posits his own
methodology to counter the misconceptions present in the writings of
European historians. This attempt makes Naumani's approach to Islamic
history inherently comparative and philosophically responsive to the
question of representation of Islam by the Europeans. In his poetry and
prose Naumani responds to European works and highlights the importance
of the history of the *ummah* and the significance of its revival in the
modern age. Naumani's pan-Islamic emphasis stems not only from his
imagination but also from personal experience. Aziz Ahmad writes:

> [Naumani] visited Istanbul in 1893; received a medal from Abd-al-Hamid
> II...and was first one of Sayyid Ahmad Khan's associates to establish contacts
> with the legendary Jamal al din al-Afghani's co-worker and disciple, Shykh
> Muhammad Abduh, in Cairo. (77)

Because of his pan-Islamic experiences, his poetry is equally as utilitarian
as Hali's, but his language is more ornate, his politics more explicit, and
his source of Muslim revival strictly Islamic.[3] It is important to note that
in later canonization of Urdu literature, Naumani is never really canonized
as a poet but rather as a historian and religious scholar, but he inhabits
both these subjectivities. I will here briefly touch upon some of Naumani's
important poems to highlight the political nature of his poetry and its
pan-Islamic vision. In a 1924 preface to Naumani's *Kuliyat-e-Shibli*
(collected Urdu poetry), Sayyid Suleman Nadwi, the editor, informs us:

> Even though Maulana's [Naumani] intellectual activities included Persian and
> Urdu poetry, he never considered himself to be a poet. (b)

Nadwi also informs us that Naumani was only an occasional poet, and wrote poetry more in response to real-life events. This assertion indicates that Naumani was mostly a public poet, who wrote poetry, as we will see, as a response to major political, social or religious issues of his time. His poetry, therefore, is very topical and contextual. This is quite obvious in his *Kuliyat*, which includes at least 53 political poems. The significance of these poems lies in the particularity of their intended audience. All the poems deal specifically with Muslim issues including issues as diverse as the Balkan War, loyalist policies of the All-India Muslim League, and the role of Muslims in the First World War.[4] The diverse range of Naumani's occasional poetry suggests that the Muslim Urdu poetry of his time had become more specific to the plight of the Muslims. The focus had shifted from loyalist apologies to the question of local and global involvement of Muslims with the European colonial powers.

Like Hali, Naumani also wrote a *Musaddas* titled: *Spectacles of Loss: A Qaumi Musaddas*.[5] It is a much shorter poem than Hali's; comprising of only sixteen six-line stanzas. Naumani recited it at a public meeting organized by the Sir Sayyid Theatre at Aligarh[6] in 1894. As the gathering was a theatrical event in which the faculty of the MAO College participated in various disguises, Naumani focuses most of his verses on the theatricality of the event itself, and then moves on to relate it to the Islamic past and present. The poem, therefore, moves from the Muslim Indian particular to the past Muslim universal—the *ummah*—and then falls back to the particularities of Indian Muslims. The use of the term *qaumi* in the title is also instructive, for it is a specific address to the Muslim *qaum* (nation) of India. After invoking the theatrical nature of the event itself, Naumani addresses his immediate audience:

Alas, the *qaum* is in such dire straits
Like a near-death patient
Without a doctor or a care-giver
Imbued with all signs of a sudden demise
And as the *quam* gets ready to die, you
Are still not satiated with the love of the spectacle. (*Kuliyat* p. 21)

This self-reflexive immediacy of the poem indicates that for Naumani, even the presentation of the *qaum's* (nation) plight has turned into a spectacle, instead of it being a reminder of the deteriorating Muslim situation. For Naumani, therefore, the irony of a staged event to represent the state of the Muslims of India has been lost on the audience who are there simply to enjoy the *tamasha* (show). He then moves on to the participants of the event and reading their particular guises as real, suggests:

> The leaders and helpers of the nation
> have now become actors on the stage (21)

Naumani then takes his audience back to the glories of the Islamic past:

> Though we try our best to forget it, but
> We sometimes do recall the glories of this nation
> There was a time when wherever we passed
> The kings and nobles walked alongside of us
> We once wiped out Caesar from Rome
> And caused great upheavals in Europe (22)

There are some obvious differences in the retrieval strategies of Hali and Naumani. While Hali, steeped in the loyalist discourse of his times, focused mainly on the social transformative history of Islam and its mastery of knowledge, Naumani's focus is more on the illustrious martial tradition of Islam. His heroes of the past are Muslim warriors who sacked empires, and changed the world, and as is evident from these lines, 'Received the throne and crown of *Kisra*⁷/And collected revenues from the Tartars' (22).

This is the lost history that Naumani hopes to retrieve, which is quite consistent with the emphasis of his historical works about the life of the Prophet Muhammad (PBUH), the second Muslim Caliph Umer-ibn-Khittaab, and his occasional pieces about Muslim heroes. In Naumani's view, then, Muslim revival cannot just be accomplished by encouraging the youth to obtain Western education: this national revival depends on retrieving and foregrounding the Muslim past, a past that brings to life the action-oriented histories of the Muslim heroes. While Naumani's audience is specifically the Indian Muslims, his sources of historical retrieval are global and rely on the history of the Muslim *ummah*. He links his audience i.e. the Indian Muslims, to the pan-Islamic world of the past, present, and future. It is this emphasis on the resistant Muslim subject, as opposed to the loyalist apologetics of the All-India Muslim League, that causes Naumani to be extremely critical of the political activities of the Muslim League.

Naumani is also caught up in local and global events impacting the political fortunes of Muslims all over the world, especially the Balkan War. This two-pronged view of reality, the global and the local plight of the

Muslims, is one major aspect of Naumani's later poetry. Being a traditionalist and an occasional poet, his poetry represents Muslim political realities against both, the British and the Hindu majority of India. Spencer Lavan captures this changed political climate as follows:

> The Partition of Bengal in 1905 had given Muslims a majority population in one province, while Morley-Minto reforms had supported the Muslim League's call for a separate electorate for Muslims.... Tensions between Hindus and Muslims had already been rising, particularly in the Punjab and Bengal where Muslims were in a majority. The political involvement of militant Arya Samaj in the Punjab as early as the 1890s was one factor leading to the communal disturbances of 1907.... The international issues of the Balkan War and the Italian invasion of Tripoli (both seen as Christian campaigns against Muslim peoples) showed increasing evidence of anti-Government feeling and growing communalism among Muslims in 1912 and 1913.

It is this confluence of global and local political events that informs Naumani's poetry of the time. In this process the Urdu poetry moves from its reformative emphasis—(Hali and Azad)—and becomes engaged with political events directly. While Hali and Azad focused on educational reform in order to create room for Muslims is the British system of rewards, Naumani's political context pushes the poetry to be overtly political and responsive to the political realities around him. In such circumstances, when the Muslim masses had become politically active, a poetry steeped in the language of loyalism was no longer tenable. In Naumani, then, we see the poet's attempt to write poetry more in touch with the current politics of his time.

To elucidate my point, I will now focus on two of Naumani's poems that deal with two important issues—one global and the other local. His poem, *Shahr Ashub*[8]*-e-Islam* (The Events of Tripoli and Balkan) was occasioned by the above cited historical events. The poem is addressed to both, the Muslims and their invaders. To the Muslims, he is attempting to highlight the extent of this new European onslaught, and to the invaders, their lust of conquest. The poem begins with a set of questions:

> If the tunic of our empire has been shredded
> For how long would its pieces fly in the sky?
> We lost Morocco and Persia, let us see
> For how long would this Turkish patient last?
> This flood that is rising in the Balkans
> How long will the wails of victims hold it? (*Kuliyat* 49)

In the first few verses, Naumani captures what the *ummah* has already lost to the West, and what they may lose as a result of the Balkan War. The war for Naumani is not an isolated event but is intricately linked to the long history of Muslim capitulations to the West. The Muslims of India, Naumani's audience, are not detached from it. This global pan-Islamic sympathy is not only a cultural trope in an occasional poem; it is rather a global political event to which the political fortunes of the Indian Muslims are linked. This sympathy places the articulation of Muslim nationhood beyond the territorial borders of India, for Naumani captures here the very nature of the global Muslim political system that has lost way to several invasions of the West.

In the next set of verses, Naumani addresses the European invaders of Tripoli and the Balkan War, but is it fairly easy to guess that he is placing these new wars within the context of other Western acts of aggression against Islam. What also comes across quite clearly is a critique of the Western lust for power and riches. The questions are, therefore, geared more towards confronting the imperial powers and speculating about the limits of their quest for power and wealth. Here is how Naumani posits these questions:

> We ask, O you teachers of human civilization
> For how long these cruelties…these atrocities?
> We know you must test the sharpness of your swords
> But for how long would you test them on our necks?
> For how long will you avenge Ayubi's[9] victories?
> For how long will you re-enact the crusades?

This questioning of the imperial powers, which includes the British, is articulated at two levels: the plane of Western claim to civilization and the plane of historical precedence. The poem, thus, confronts the very normalizing narrative of the colonial powers and their claim to be the custodians of the new civilization. Hence, the first ironic line questions these 'teachers' about the atrocities that they continue committing under the banner of progress and a civilizing mission. Also, the reference to the crusades links the current wars as an extension to medieval European adventurism. What comes across in the poem is this new voice of the native subject: the questioning subject that was missing in the poetry of Hali and Azad. The focus is no longer on the failures of Muslims but also on the excesses of the colonizers. In the concluding verses of the poem, Naumani returns to his Muslim audience as he explains the possible consequences of this new European onslaught on the Muslim world:

The pages of the book of Islam are being scattered
For how long would these winds of *kuf'r* last?
For they may, if they continue like this
Touch the fabric of the *haram* (50)

Thus, the final message of the poem is that the global persecution of the Muslim has now reached a level where it cannot be contained, and it has now started threatening the very core of the Muslim world: the *Haram* (Holy Kaaba). In this brief poem, occasioned by real-life global events, Naumani articulates the anxieties of the Indian Muslims, anxieties that are extra-territorial and Pan-Islamic. The lesson that we may learn from this is that the local troubles of the Muslims of India are not isolated and that whatever happens to the Muslims elsewhere has a direct impact on the lives of Indian Muslims. In this connection with the global, Naumani is able to articulate the voice of the Muslim subject, who is no longer satisfied with the strategy of loyalism, and who must express his political concerns in more unequivocal terms.

This particular aspect of Muslim criticism of the British elite is even more explicitly articulated in yet another poem occasioned by a local event, namely, the Kanpur Mosque incident of 1913. The incident, as reported in a British official's telegram to the Private Secretary to the Viceroy of India, is narrated by Spencer Lavan:

Mass meeting of Muhammadans held Eedgah this morning. On conclusion marched with black flags flying to mosque and commenced rebuilding demolished portion[10] and throwing stones at *kotwal* and other police present.... Magistrate ordered police to fire. Failing to prevent mob advancing, Superintendent police and *kotwal* led charge of mounted police and forced rioters back. Armed police then cleared surroundings of mosque. All quiet before noon. Probably between twenty and thirty rioters killed and wounded. (263)

Lavan also traces the communal impact of this incident on the Muslim consciousness, especially, as it was reported by the Muslim journals. One of the most influential responses to the incident was Naumani's poem occasioned by the tragedy of Kanpur, which, according to Nadwi, was published in the pages of Urdu journals: such as *Hamdard, Muslim Gazzette, Zamindar*, and *Al Hilal*. The poem, in Nadwi's words: 'became the most popular poem for the Muslim masses' (68). The poem entitled 'We are the Dead of Kanpur', addresses the reader through the voices of the people killed during the Kanpur massacre. From the very first line the narrator shows us the demographic breakdown of dead or dying victims: children, the young men, and the aged. We learn that they had all come to Kanpur to 'stop the lances on their chests,' (69) to save the Machli Bazar Mosque. In the last line, when asked about who they are, the dead reply: 'we are the dead of Kanpur' (69). The Persian term *Kushtagan-e-Kanpur* that Naumani has chosen for his description of the dead is quite instructive, for it highlights the degree of brutality involved in the massacre. They are the *Kushtagan-e-Kanpur,* the ones who were murdered at Kanpur, and since they died defending a mosque, the incident is a purely Muslim incident that puts the Muslim–English relationship in a whole new light. These Muslims did not die in a general riot; they were killed while defending a sacred Muslim place of worship, a mosque. He also links the particular plight of the Kanpur Muslims to their international counterparts in another brief poem. It reads:

> Why is it that the numbers of Arab prophet's people keep on decreasing
> It is because they keep on being killed from Balkans to Kanpur (72-3).

Hence, in these victims of Kanpur, who are part of the global chain of Muslim annihilation, Naumani can retrieve the kind of Muslims he idealized, the man of action ready to die for his cause. His poetry, with such immediacy and pathos, is much different from that of Hali and his cohorts; it attempts to transform the Muslim masses into people of action to rise in opposition to an obvious atrocity being committed against Islam and the Muslims. And no amount of Westernized education can accomplish such a transformation; it must spring from within the well of Islamic tradition, the source Naumani considered as the only means for the revival of Islamic prestige and fortune. It seems the tables have turned, and the Muslims, at least those sympathetic to Naumani's thought process, must confront the British on unapologetic and confrontational terms.

Another issue that troubled Naumani were the attempts by the Arya Samajists to reconvert newly converted Muslims back to Hinduism. Naumani then must also, besides highlighting the issue of Muslim identity in opposition to the British, particularize the Muslims in difference with the Hindus. In an article, included in *Makalat-e-Shibli* (13 April 1908, Vol. 8), Naumani broaches this particular issue:

> The religious aggression of the Aryans [Arya Samaj] has been quite beneficial to the Muslim cause, even though they have been able to convert a few Muslims to Hinduism through their treachery and through abductions. This has lit a fire from one corner of Hindustan to the other. The Muslims have

suddenly been jolted from their sleep, especially the group that had abandoned religious education for the sake of worldly education.... We must explore the reasons for these conversions. In my opinion, the only reason for this reversal is that these people were completely ignorant of Islamic articles of faith, Islamic precepts, and Islamic history. This is all because of the extreme emphasis on worldly education.... We are not opposed to worldly education—we want every Muslim child to have it—but we must also spend all our energies in imparting religious education. We should build a great Muslim institution where we can teach the students all possible branches of religious knowledge. (3-4)

The Arya Samaj was established by Swami Dayanand in 1875 (Wadhwa 3), and it was their attempts at converting the Rajput Muslims back to Hinduism that prompted the above cited essay by Naumani. What is more important for my argument is the way Naumani employs this new threat to the Muslims of India: he uses it to make a case for a more traditional Islamic education. As stated earlier, for Naumani, any idea of Muslim revival was inherently linked with traditional Islam. He uses the Arya Samaj activities to bolster his claim about the importance of religious education. Hence, to save the Muslim future, the education of the Muslim youth must include religious education along with their secular education. In a nutshell, for the Muslims to survive against an onslaught of the Hindu revivalists, a grand institution is needed where Muslim youth can be trained in the disciplines peculiar to their faith. It is important to note here that Naumani is appealing for the need of an institution of higher education and not just a *madrassa*. His dream will eventually materialize and play an important role in creating the kind of leadership Naumani desired for the Muslim youth. For my discussion here it is important to note that Naumani, through his poetry and journalism, is now responding to a two-pronged threat posed by the Hindus and the British. The question of Muslim particularity and exceptionalism is no longer a case of winning British patronage through loyalty; it has now become confrontational. With these political imperatives, for Naumani, Muslim survival can no longer be ensured by the loyalist apologetics: Muslims must return to their traditions to claim their particular place within India. As is obvious from this discussion, Naumani's ideas did not stem from some kind of an inner, detached genius: he was a product of his times and his works encompass the changed socio-political imperatives. While he still articulates the Muslim particularity within the British Indian context, his work is produced in a changed political context. The Muslims are no longer simply fighting for survival within India, and their vision is not simply focused on the plight of Indian Muslims. Political events, both local and global, have transformed the politics of literary production for a large group of Muslim scholars and poets who now find it imperative to question British global and local policies, while, at the same time, also challenging the purely loyalist strategies of Sayyid Ahmad Khan and his followers.

While Naumani may be classified as the scholar poet of his times, Akbar Allahabadi, on the other hand, was a neo-traditionalist satirist who made any attempts at uncritical loyalism a constant subject of his satire. I will now move on to discuss briefly his contribution to the critique of loyalism. Ali Jawad Zaidi provides us with the following brief account of Akbar Allahabadi's life:

> Syed Akbar Hussain Akbar Allahabadi (1846–1921), was sent to the Jamuna Mission High School after his early education at home. He left the school without doing his matriculation and entered government service in 1863, taking up different jobs as a copyist, reader, and finally a *Tehsildar*, he joined the Bar and became an officiating Munsif in 1880. Nine years later he was raised to sub-judgeship. He died a broken man in 1921, after prolonged illness and the loss of his loving wife and young son. (281)

There seems to be nothing spectacular in this brief portrayal of Allahabadi's life: a British subject who rose to the highest level that someone of his background could have risen to within the British Indian Services. But what makes Allahabadi one of the most enduring poets of his time is his great wit and criticism of the British and the British loyalists. While being a true example of an ideal British dependent, Allahabadi is one of the most incisive critics of the British (Western) system of education, and the apologetics of the loyalists. It is his satirical poetry that has kept him alive in the Muslim imagination long after his death. Calling him the first of the Muslim nationalists, Jamil Jalibi[11] opines the following about Akbar Allahabadi:

> People usually think Akbar Allahabadi was just a humorist, which is partially true. But humour for Allahabadi was a means to pass his message on to people. There was something completely new in Akbar's poetry, something not seen in any of his contemporaries. Having seen the dominance of the British in India... Akbar could see that against such an onslaught the Muslims will lose their own system of civilization and become complete slaves of the Western civilization... Hence, while Sir Sayyid Ahmad Khan was the leader of the new [Westernized] generation, Akbar was the spokesperson for the *ulama* and devout Muslims. (1)

What becomes quite evident from the above passage is that Akbar Allahabadi's anxieties about the Muslims of India were not much different from that of Shibli Naumani; only he chose to express them through his humorist poetry, a poetry more prone to being popularized. What Jamil Jalibi points out above is extremely important. In his poetry, Akbar Allahabadi is able to highlight a very important aspect of East–West exchange, which is pertinent in understanding the postcolonial history of Pakistan. A total adoption of secular education, in his view, weakens the traditional bases of Muslim identity and pride. What comes out of a completely secular and Westernized educational process is a subject completely immersed in the Western ideals possessing only a superficial knowledge of his own particular history. In Akbar Allahabadi's view, which corresponds to those of Naumani's, this total surrender of one's own heritage is a recipe for perpetual subjugation. It is because of this particular aspect of Allahabadi's poetry that I have included a brief discussion of his works.

I will briefly discuss some of Allahabadi's popular poetry to highlight his contribution to the idea of Muslim particularity from a neo-traditionalist perspective. In a poem translated and cited by Muhammad Sadiq, Allahabadi opines about the moral condition of Indian Muslims:

The direction of the breeze indicates a change in the season;
New flowers (evil) will now blossom and the song of the nightingale will be heard less and less.
Old faiths will dwindle and die on account of religious reforms;
There will be a new Ka'ba and Western statues will be the idols.
No one will feel this change nor be sorry at it,
They will all be the notes of the new harp that gave them birth.
Why should you break your heart over this revolution O Akbar!
The time is quite near when neither you nor I shall be here. (311)

Muhammad Sadiq places these verses in Akbar's 'didactic mode' (311) a method meant to highlight the impact of new Westernization on the Muslim faith. What is also peculiar about these verses is the acute specificity of their symbols and audience. The audience is specifically Muslim and the symbols invoked are clearly Islamic. The reference to the Ka'ba is extremely important, for the last time that the Ka'ba was literally adorned with idols was during the life of the Prophet himself when the Quresh of Makkah in the seventh century were its custodians. The most moving accounts of the Prophet's return to Makkah after thirteen years of exile are those of the final cleansing of the Ka'ba. Hence, to Akbar, what is happening in India is a recurrence of the same idolatry, only this time it is led by the Europeans. On the whole, the poem expresses the deep loss experienced by the Muslims of India in the name of reform and a new system of thought.

With such views about Western education and influence upon the Muslims, Akbar Allahabadi finds a perfect target in Sir Sayyid's loyalism. Here is another brief poem on this topic, translated and quoted by Iqbal Hussain:

> O Akbar, if I remain firm in my old ways,
> The Saiyid says plainly that this attitude [lit. colour]
> is tarnished.
> And if I adopt the modern ways, then my own community
> raises such a hue and cry.
> If I speak of moderation then this is not well received
> on either side.
> All of them have spread out their legs beyond limit.
> One is adamant so as not to touch even lemonade;
> While the other cries out for wine and cup.
> On one side, there is motive and interest,
> On the other, a postbag containing Revelations from Britain. (32)

As is pretty obvious, this is a wonderful comparison of the two strands of Muslim politics: the neo-traditionalists and the assimilationist/loyalists. Allahabadi finds both groups to be overstretched and caught in the extremes. While the Westernized elite have completely adopted British ways—the Revelations—the traditionalists consider even the harmless aspects of the West as dangerous to their religion. This is the same anxiety that Nazeer Ahmad expressed in his novels, the problem of complete Muslim distrust of the new ways. But Allahabadi is also hinting at something important: the extreme reluctance of both the groups to find a middle ground. It is here that his thought coincides with that of Naumani. Just as Naumani wanted the native Muslim youth to be as conversant with their own heritage as that of the West, Allahabadi also seeks such a balanced approach. As Sayyid Ahmad Khan's approach, because of his absolute faith in the British system, fails to qualify as a balanced approach, he is, therefore, seen as a less positive influence.

On the whole, in Akbar Allahabadi and Shibli Naumani, we see a trend opposed to what had been the dominant aspect of Muslim politics since post-rebellion times. They express a critique of the extreme loyalism of the Loyalist group and the politics of the embryonic Indian Muslim League. It is in their works that one can finally retrieve the canonical speaking subject of postcolonial scholarship: the subject of resistance. But as I have suggested earlier, this does not imply that the politics of loyalism are replaced by the language of resistance. Both Naumani and Allahabadi also end up particularizing the Muslim identity in the Indian as well as the pan-Islamic context. Hence, even though both these strands develop simultaneously and sometimes overlap, the final outcome is invariably always an expression of Muslim exceptionalism. What we learn in the process is that the Muslim literary production was more complex and never monolithic in its contact with colonialism. This discussion leads me to the most important Muslim literary figure of the twentieth century, the one who, somehow, combines these two strands of Muslim thought and offers the most formidable philosophical challenge to the dominant West: Allama Sir Muhammad Iqbal.

NOTES

1. Shibli is more famous for his religious works, especially his ambitious attempt at writing the most comprehensive biography of the Prophet Muhammad (PBUH). I will here focus mostly on his poetry with occasional references to his religious works.
2. All citations from Shibli Naumani's works, unless otherwise stated, are in my translation.
3. By this I mean that Naumani does not consider western education as the sole means of changing the condition of the Muslims of India. In his view, the Muslims of India can succeed only by recovering their past and by maintaining their traditional Islamic values.
4. As Naumani died in 1914 there is only one poem about the First World War.
5. This is a fairly free translation of the title. The important noun that Naumani uses in the title is *ibrat*, which means looking at the past to learn about one's mistakes.
6. Sayyid Suleman Nadwi informs us that this particular event was organised by Sayyid Ahmad Khan in 1894 under the particular theme of *Tamasha-e-Ibrat* (Spectacle of Loss). In this event all major figures associated with Sir Sayyid's movement dressed up in various costumes to present the state of affairs of the Muslims of India through their costumes and the public recitation of their works.
7. *Kisra* is the Persian term for the Persian dynasty that the early Arab invaders defeated in the eighth century CE.
8. In Urdu and Persian poetry *Shahr Ashub* is a specific genre of tragic poetry written about the destruction or loss of a Muslim city. Naumani is expanding the scope of this particular genre to include two theatres of war affecting the Muslims.
9. A reference to the military victories of Sultan Salah-ud-Din Ayubi against the crusaders.

10. According to Lavan's research, the portion of the Machli Bazar mosque had already been demolished to make room for a road-broadening project. This procession was, therefore, organised to rebuild the demolished portion.

11. All citations from Jamil Jalibi are in my translation.

6

Allama Muhammad Iqbal: Challenging the Master's Narrative

It is impossible to cover the vast scope and philosophical depth of Iqbal's works in one chapter. Even Annemarie Schimmel, probably the most prominent Western scholar on Iqbal, admits, 'It is difficult to build up a system from Iqbal's works (229). The mere scope of his work[1] makes it impossible to give any definitive explanation of his thoughts or interests.[2] I will, therefore, restrict my discussion of Iqbal to his views of the politics of the West and his articulation of the idea of Muslim nationhood.[3]

Iqbal inhabits the very subjectivity that Shibli Naumani expected to see in the Muslims of his time: he is a poet who possesses a deeper knowledge of his own tradition and history along with a formidable knowledge of Western systems of thought, history and politics. In Frantz Fanon's terms, then, he is a poet who can compose 'the sentence which expresses the heart of the people' (223). This is what Fanon calls the 'the third phase... the fighting phase [in which] the native, after having tried to lose himself in the people and with the people, will on the contrary shake the people' (222). Iqbal, thus, is the intellectual in the fighting phase of the nation. Just as nationalism for Fanon is a path to an Africa beyond the nation; so is the state of the Indian Muslims for Iqbal. There is not even a single verse in Iqbal's Persian and Urdu poetry that favours territorial nationalism, yet in his political life, as discussed in the next chapter, he articulates a vision of a future Muslim nation-state. In Fanon's views, 'national consciousness, which is not nationalism, is the only thing that will give us an international dimension' (247). Hence, nation for Fanon is a staging point for launching an African humanism. For Iqbal, the Muslim Identity is inherently transnational and trans-historical, and he returns to the nation—in his prose work—only if the nation eventually promises to fulfil its pan-Islamic purpose. In this chapter I will only concern myself with Iqbal's views about the West in general, and about nationalism in particular. But first, a brief overview of Iqbal's life that should inform us about the material circumstances within which Iqbal produced his works.

According to Hafeez Malik and Lynda P. Malik, Iqbal was born in Sialkot, Pakistan, on 9 November 1877. Iqbal received his early education at Scotch Mission College (now Murray College), and then moved to Lahore to study English literature, Arabic, and Philosophy at Government College, Lahore. After completing his Masters, Iqbal left for Europe in 1905 for advanced graduate studies. In London, he studied at Lincoln's Inn to qualify for the Bar, and also enrolled as an undergraduate at Trinity College. During the same period he also submitted a dissertation to Munich University and was granted a Doctorate. During the period of his early education, his main influence came from Maulvi Mir Hassan, a teacher of Persian literature at Scotch Mission College, while at Government College, Lahore, Iqbal benefited from the personal attention of Thomas Arnold, a renowned orientalist of his time (3-20).

This brief introduction clarifies the very particularity of Iqbal's experiences: he grows up in times when, depending upon one's resources, opting for a secular education is no longer a contested terrain. Also, in his case he is exposed to what could be termed the best of both worlds: his early education is overseen by the likes of Maulvi Mir Hassan who was deeply aware of the Muslim literary tradition and heritage; while in his college years Iqbal was able to benefit from the tutelage of Thomas Arnold.[4] Hence, it can be said that both the East and the West combined to form Iqbal's subjectivity. The immediate cultural and political context also plays an important role in defining Iqbal's literary production.

Iqbal, as Annemarie Schimmel informs us, was born 'the very year that Aligarh [University] was beginning to function' (223). He matures into a poet after people like Naumani and Akbar Allahabadi have already developed a tradition of critiquing the loyalist policies of the Muslim League, in a Muslim India that has already witnessed the Balkan War and the Italian invasion of Tripoli. This is also the time when the Muslim cultural centre—through the efforts of Hali and Azad—has shifted to Lahore. So this is the Lahore scenario that Iqbal enters to study at the Government College. Hafeez and Lynda Malik describe this cultural milieu as follows:

> In the last decade of the nineteenth century a Musha'ra (poetical symposium) was regularly organised in the *Bazaar Hakiman* inside *Bhati Gate* of the walled city of Lahore....*Bhati Gate* was then the center of Lahore's intellectual and cultural activities. Students of local colleges often came, sometimes to enjoy

the recitation of poetry, sometimes to compete as budding poets. Iqbal was...lured to the poetical symposia of *Bhati Gate*. (11)

This was the popular space where Iqbal was, for the first time, recognized for his poetical talent. Iqbal's poetry, therefore, from its very beginning is linked to the people. Lahore being a majority Muslim city, and the emphasis on Urdu in the *mushairahs* in itself makes Iqbal the popular voice of his people, the Muslims. These early experiences define the Iqbal of the future: A poet constantly in conversation with his people, a poet attempting to retrieve a Muslim self to counter the overwhelming ideological onslaught of the West. It is this public imperative that forces Iqbal to articulate a peculiar view about the West and prompts a deep introspective study of Islam itself. It is within these two important points of reference that the idea of Muslim particularity takes shape in Iqbal's works. About Iqbal's views on the West, Khalifa Abdul Hakim[5] suggests: 'This tendency to criticize the West is so deeply embedded in Iqbal's thoughts that in so many of his poems, even if it is completely out of place, he will insert one odd critical strike at the West. (201)

Iqbal, unlike Sayyid Ahmad and his loyalists, takes it upon himself to complicate the benevolent view of the West by highlighting its darker side. It is, however, important to note that Iqbal's view of East and the West is not always binaristic, though he does sometimes rely on a binarisitc structure to make a point. For him the question is not that of choosing between East and West, but rather to find a middle ground where Muslims do not have to abandon their Islamic identity to be part of the modern world. Most occasional critical references in his poetry to the West must, therefore, be read within this context. Iqbal critiques and indicts certain specific aspects of the West that include imperialism, secularism, materialism, class system etc. Iqbal places his hopes in the individual rather than the large systems of East and West, which can be clearly seen in the concluding lines of his Persian work *Javid Nama*:

> Be not enchanted by the West
> Nor on the East thou needest dote,
> For both this ancient and this new
> Together are not worth an oat.
> Alone live thou, with all tread well.
> Than radiant sun that illumines
> The ancient sky thou art more bright
> So live that every grain of sand
> May borrow brilliance from thy light. (186-187)

There are two major categories in which Iqbal places the East and West: East is the world of *man* (heart) while West is the world of *tan* (body). Also, the driving force of the East is *Ishq* (love) while the main driving force of the West is *Aql* (intellect). It is within this framework of *man* and *ishq*; *tan* and *aql* that Iqbal discusses the East–West dilemma. What is important about this particular description is that within this framework, Iqbal can posit a claim of the East's contribution to the West, for unless a civilization possesses both sets of values, it is not a viable civilization for the modern world. Strategically, this philosophical stance allows Iqbal to make the East–West exchange a reciprocal one in which both can share their core values to create a better world. This division of internal and external attributes also allows Iqbal to create room for offering an alternative world view. Iqbal, therefore, does not seek the Muslim response to the British within the private realm but by articulating and foregrounding the importance of Islam and the *ummah* as a political system. This focus on the *ummah* also had its material reasons, which Francis Robinson explains as follows:

> The reasons for this expanding vision were, of course, many: the impact of colonial rule; the realization that the encroachment of the West was an experience being shared by almost all Muslims; the increasing ease with which Muslims were able to travel to be with Muslims in other lands; the need to find a sense of identity as they grappled with the meaning of the modern state in colonial form. (243)

Unlike Hali and Sir Sayyid, for Iqbal, the Muslim future does not simply depend on gaining Western knowledge but also by balancing this knowledge with their own traditions. Iqbal's own work displays this engagement with the West: It is always mediated through his knowledge of both these systems. The categories of *man* and *ishq* and *tan* and *aql* become a litmus test for including certain aspects of Western knowledge into Eastern thought; hence, if a Western philosopher or leader displays an understanding of the concept of *man* and *ishq*, then he/she, somehow, inhabits the spirit of the East and can be included as an honorary member of the world of the heart.[6] It is also within these categories that Iqbal at times seeks true freedom from the constraints of imperialism and convention. He broaches this subject in one of his *ghazals* form *Baal-e-Jibreel*.[7]

> The world of heart is a world of feeling and passion
> The world of body is a world of profit, loss and treachery

When you have the world of heart, it cannot be lost
The world of body is like a shadow, here now and then gone
In the world of heart I never encountered the Raj of *Afrangi*[8]
In the world of heart I never found the Sheikh and Brahmin. (*Baal-e-Jibreel* 323)

Iqbal is not attempting to privilege the private sphere over the public sphere: his Muslim hero[9] is a man of action and a man of the world, but his approach to the world is non-materialistic. According to Iqbal, it is through introspection and love that one may achieve absolute freedom. If one were to focus on strengthening one's spiritual self, then there are no fears of political dominance of the *afrangi* or the religious control of the clergy. Hence, the Sheikh and the Brahmin (Hindu and Muslim clergy) will have no sway over a person who defines life from within. True freedom is experienced through the soul, not through one's flesh. Iqbal concludes the poem with a message:

It shamed me to hear these words from a *Qalandar*[10]
When you bow in front of the other
You have neither the *man* nor the *tan* (323).

It is this dependence on the mercy of others that robs one of one's entire self: the body and the heart. Hence, a colonial relationship of dependence on the *afrangi* is a relationship of loss of one's self. After this brief discussion of Iqbal's concept of Self, I shall now briefly discuss one of his most comprehensive poems on the West.

Published posthumously in 1938, the poem titled *Iblees ki Majlis-e-Shura* (The Parliament of Satan) is a scathing criticism of the major socio-political and economic systems offered by the West. The poem's immediate historical context is extremely important: it was written after the First World War and the Russian Revolution. In the Islamic world, the Caliphate has been abolished and Mustafa Kemal has already put Turkey on a secular path. Within the context of Indian politics, the All-India Muslim League has been revived by Jinnah and despite its recent electoral setbacks, it is considered a major Muslim political party. Iqbal, by this time is reaching the end of his illustrious career, and has already expressed, in 1930, his vision of a future Muslim homeland.

The poem is organized as a discussion between Satan and his advisors. While Satan boasts of his accomplishments, his advisors remind him of various threats to his system. Satan refutes all their claims of the dangers one by one but then goes on to speculate about the possibility of one final threat. This threat that could undo Satan's entire world is the resurgence of Islam. In the process of this discussion, Iqbal brings up all the major challenges—mostly Western systems—to Satan's world-system and it is in these challenges that Iqbal articulates the bankruptcy of various Western systems of governance and socio-economic control. The opening lines of the poems are a self-congratulatory statement by Satan:

> I showed the *Farangi* the dream of Kingship
> I broke the spell of the Church and the Mosque
> I taught the poor the lesson of fate
> I gave the rich the madness of capitalism
> Who can dowse this raging fire?
> That blazes with the vigour of *Iblees*.[11] (*Armughan-e-Hijaz* 647)

Satan is referring to the existing world; a world already arranged according to his design.[12] The system that he has created includes all the major accomplishments of humankind: the systems of government, the religions, and people's place in this system. The Urdu/Persian term used for kingship is *malukiyat*, (which means a system of absolute monarchy) and which Satan claims as his own. He also claims having destroyed the love for any metaphysical explanation of reality, hence the Western emphasis on secularism. But this rationalism has not eliminated, at least in the Muslim world, a belief in fate, in predestination, which is an ideal tool for keeping the poor locked in their place. Thus, wherever necessary the poor are kept resigned to their fate while the rich are imbued with greed to produce wealth, mostly for their own good. This world that Satan has created—the world as it exists—depends on systems that keep humankind divided and sundered from God, and is, therefore, an ideal world for the work of Satan.

Upon this declaration of Satan his first adviser agrees with him and provides evidence in favour of Satan's declaration. Most of the supporting evidence provided comes from the Muslim world. This system, the adviser suggests, has made the Sufis and mullahs into spokespersons of kings: it is because the Sufis teach people an impractical withdrawal from the world and the mullahs, in Iqbal's views, teach people about the doctrine of *taqdeer*, fate, that cannot be altered. With such views of reality, the Muslim masses can never attempt to change things, for such misguided teachings have convinced them that it is their destiny to endure the present for a better hereafter. Iqbal here is referring to the major debates in Islamic theology about the issue of *taqdeer*; in his own poetry human beings are dynamic and have the capacity to create their own destiny. The adviser's final words about the Muslims declare that the current state of Islam is ideal for the Satan's system because 'Their Swords have rusted/and Jihad has been forbidden' (649). But then the second adviser, a sceptic, asks of the first: 'Is it good or bad, this noise about the rule of the people/ Or are you not aware of the new troubles of the world?' (649). At this the First adviser replies:

> I am aware, but my knowledge of the world tells me
> There is no danger if it is another form of *malukiyat*
> We have ourselves garbed kingship in a popular dress
> When Humans became a little self-aware
> Haven't you seen the popular system of the West?
> Bright-faced with a heart darker than Changez. (649-50)

The last two lines refer to the rise of democracy in the West, which is seen by the Devil's adviser as a potent threat to his system. The response of the first advocate resonates with Iqbal's own views on Western democracy. Elsewhere, Iqbal has defined democracy as 'the same old organ/imbued with the tune of kings' (*Baang-e-Dara* 261). What this poem is trying to convey is that the prevailing democracy is not really a serious threat to Satan's plans since, for the masses it is simply another form of kingship in another garb whose essence is darker than its appearance. Iqbal justifies his emphasis on it being dark for two reasons: its gross capitalism, and its lack of religious spirit. In the words of Khalifa Abdul Hakim: 'Iqbal is ambivalent about Western democracy' (281). He further goes on to explain that in Iqbal's views: 'True democracy was represented by early Islam, in which there was no ruling class and the state was a welfare state' (287). The reason why the prevailing Western democracy cannot be a threat to Satan is because it has failed to eliminate class-division, and the elite are now privileged under the banner of the people. The present system is Satanic also because of the inherent inequality and exploitative nature of capitalism itself. For Iqbal, this democracy is also dual-faced, for it shows one face in the West, and another, darker face in the colonies. A third advocate talks here of another philosophy of the West:

> But what's the answer to the mischief of that wise Jew
> That Moses without light…that cross-less Jesus
> Not a prophet, but with a book under his arm
> For what could be more dangerous than this
> That the serfs uproot the tents of their masters. (650)

This is obviously a reference to Karl Marx. We are now being presented with another alternative by the West in the form of Socialism, which is opposed to class-division of a capitalistic society, but it involves the annihilation of the masters at the hands of the people. Certainly this could destroy the inherent duplicity of the capitalistic democracy. But Iqbal's views on Marx and socialism are also quite ambivalent: He finds Marx's message revolutionary and closest to the teachings of Islam, but is opposed to its lack of spirituality. For Iqbal, writing God out of history and replacing the Creator with a material explanation of the world is inconsistent with Islam. Khalifa Abdul Hakim suggests:

> This is the difference between Marx and Iqbal; both are out for revolution but one wants to achieve it through hatred, and the other through love. One says: Arise the workers of the world, to shatter this sorry scheme of things.... Iqbal says, Arise, ye the rich and the poor alike, and realize your real selves through love. (*Islam* 122)

Thus, Iqbal appropriates Marx to highlight the exploitative role of capitalism but imbues his socialistic ideas with an Islamic spirit. Marx's influence on Iqbal, however, is undeniable and becomes obvious in several of his poems. Some of his Persian poems about the working class in *Payam-e-Mashriq* (A Message from the East) are obviously Marxist in their tone. In 'Division between the Capitalist and the Labourer', Iqbal highlights their differences:

> Mine is the din of steel factory,
> And yours is the church organ's melody
> The earth and what is in its bowels are mine;
> From earth to heaven all is your territory. (176)

Hence, despite his ambivalence about Marxism, Iqbal finds its socialistic message much more acceptable than the class hierarchies of capitalism. However, in the poem, another one of Satan's disciples observes: 'We have found its answer in the palaces of Rome/Where Caesar's people are dreaming of Caesar again.' (651). According to this, fascism is a good enough defence against the threat of Marxism, especially if espoused by a people who intend to rekindle what they consider their ancient heritage. But Satan's parliament is not convinced with this solution. Another advocate then urges Satan to give a definitive opinion. Satan first declares: 'I am not afraid of these socialist gypsies/these itinerant, mercurial ones don't bother me' (654). 'But I do fear the *ummah* of Islam.' And this is where Iqbal, in articulating Satan's fears, inserts the problems and possibilities of the Muslim *ummah*:

> I know this *ummah* no longer holds the Qur'an
> The same capitalism is Muslim's faith.
> In the pitch-dark night of the East
> The hands of the clergy are void of light.[13]
> But the currents of the present make me fear
> That the message of the Prophet might appear again. (654)

The present-day Muslims have lost all their strength to cause a universal upheaval. They have lost their relationship with the Quran, their primary source of wisdom. The religious elite themselves are not enlightened. There is a possibility now of someone to appear to rekindle the light and the Prophet's way again. And this is what Satan actually is fearful of. He describes this system of the prophet as follows:

> Protector of women's honour, tester of men
> A message of death for all sorts of slavery
> Undivided amongst kings and beggars
> Cleans the wealth of all its filth
> Makes the rich the custodians of riches
> What could be greater than this revolution?
> Not to kings but to God belongs the land. (655)

This is Islam's classless society in which there is no ownership of land but simply custodianship. This subtle difference between the classical Marxist approach to property and that of Islam is one revolutionary concept that Iqbal also explained elsewhere in his works. In another poem from *Baal-e-Jibreel* Iqbal asserts: 'In God's name this land is neither yours nor mine/Neither it is of your ancestors or mine' (119). The poem is titled '*Al ard lillah*' which is a verse of the Qur'an meaning it is God's land. Hence, in Iqbal's view the rich cannot be owners of land, but may hold it as a trust and those who work the lands are rightful heirs of its bounties. Obviously, Satan is threatened by this ideology, for if ownership could be abolished by God's word, then the whole edifice of the economy of ownership would collapse.

In his final message Satan declares that whatever the Muslims are entangled in at the present must be perpetuated so that they do not arise and topple his carefully built system. Satan suggests a number of ways to ensure the precariousness of the situation of the Muslims:

Better he remains entangled in the mysteries of Godhead
In various interpretations of the Book of God
Keep him ignorant of the world of character
Until all his pawns are taken in the game of life
Keep him busy in the problems of day to day
Mould his moods to the temperament of Shrines. (657)

The factors that Satan considers as tools to keep the Muslim threat at bay are the very points that Iqbal and other reformers consider as the ills in Islam of their time. Iqbal is pointing towards the two extremities within the Islam of his time: over-intellectualization of faith by Muslim philosophers, and ritualization of Islam by the mullahs. Both these aspects of Islam had taken away the dynamism of Islam and replaced it with detached pedantry and superstitious rituals. For Satan, as long as the Muslims are entangled in the sectarian divide over the interpretation of the Qur'an instead of embodying its dynamic spirit, they will never be capable enough to rise against him in challenge. Similarly, the Sufi philosophy also encouraged a withdrawal from real-life and replaced it with detached spiritual rituals, hence becoming an ideal system for replacing the Muslim dynamic spirit with a sacralised ineptitude and invocation of fate to explain material realities. But Iqbal is not opposed to all forms of Sufism. Iqbal's view on Islam is that of a dynamic religion. He believes that, 'Islam says "yes" to the world of matter and points the way to master it with a view to discover a basis for a realistic regulation of life' (*Reconstruction of Religious Thought in Islam* 16). Such Sufi practices that suggested a withdrawal from the world of action to an uncontested belief in fate were, to Iqbal, against the dynamic spirit of Islam. According to Ahmad Mian Akhtar:[14] 'Iqbal had studied Islamic Sufism deeply including the original writings of all great Sufis. But he had noticed certain un-Islamic practices in Sufism and was opposed to these un-Islamic influences' (114). In one of his published letters, quoted by Mian Akhtar, Iqbal elaborates upon these un-Islamic influences:

> This Neo-Platonism is an altered version of Plato that one of his followers (Plotinus) presented as a religion. In Muslims this was spread through Christian translations and became a part of Islam. In my opinion this is strictly un-Islamic and has no relationship with the Qura'nic philosophy. The edifice of Sufism is based on this Greek absurdity. (119)

In Iqbal's view, this emphasis on neo-Platonism precipitated the decline of Muslim philosophy into a world of inaction and fate. As Iqbal's Muslim is a man of action, any system that forces a Muslim to leave the world to seek God is, therefore, not suitable for the action-oriented life expected of a Muslim. That is why Satan, in the poem under discussion, wants to keep the Muslims busy with the love of the Sufi shrines.

Through this brief discussion of Iqbal's 'The Parliament of Satan' we may deduce that Iqbal is not simply challenging the surface realities of colonialism; he also dwells on the deeper philosophical impact of the West on Islam and then attempts to offer his own philosophical remedies. The native–master relationship, it seems, has moved from apologetic loyalism to philosophical challenge and criticism.

Iqbal also considers it important to stress upon the inherent brutalities of the Western power and knowledge paradigm. In this critique of the West, the use of modern technologies of violence in the First World War forms an important backdrop. In one of his poems entitled 'The Wisdom of the West', included in his *Payam-e-Mahriq*, Iqbal elaborates upon this point. The poem includes the lament of a man who has died and is complaining to God about the manner of his death. His main complaint is that the Angel of Death is no longer at his best and needs new training. The man requests God to send the Angel of Death to the West for training:

> The West develops wonderful new skills
> In this as in so many other fields
> Its submarines are crocodiles
> Its bombers rain destruction from the skies
> Its gasses so obscure the sky
> They blind the sun's world-seeing eye.
> Dispatch this old fool to the West
> To learn the art of killing fast—and best. (90-91)

Iqbal's views on the West are obviously more strident than the staid views of early loyalists. Iqbal, though himself a product of the colonial system, does not only critique the West as a native alone; nor has he lost a sense of his own cultural identity. He is, in other words, not what Lord Macaulay had hoped for as an end-product of an English education: 'Indian in blood and colour, but English in taste, in opinions, in morals, and in intellect' (Macaulay 130); his critique of the West comes from within the Western philosophies of self-representation. In such a critique, Western liberal democracy's class hierarchies and wealth distribution is exposed. Similarly, Marxism faces its own critique in its extreme focus on the material world alone. In Iqbal's views a modern system must offer the best of all systems, and to him Islam offers such a system. The native is not just demanding inclusion within the colonial system; he is, rather, offering his own philosophical and political ideology as a solution to the problems of the colonial masters. This alternative against the dominance of the West is presented in the shape of a universal Islamic system. It is this system of politics and culture that forms the basis of his idea of a Muslim Nation.

As stated earlier, Iqbal opposes purely Western territorial nationalism. Iqbal only supports the idea of an Indian Muslim nation-state as a tactical measure, the details of which I will discuss in the next chapter. Overall, Iqbal's idea of Muslim identity is trans-historical and trans-national; he sees the Western concept of the nation-state as a divisive force against the Islamic concept of a larger Muslim *ummah*. The true centre of the Islamic world for him is the Hijaz—Makkah—and the entire history of Muslim accomplishments a common Muslim heritage. He expresses this in one of his early poems: *Tarana-e-Milli* (A National Song). A poem for schoolchildren, the following message is expressed here:

> Ours is China and Arabia, ours is Hindustan
> We are Muslims and the whole world is our country
> Our hearts contain the gift of *Tauhid*,[15]
> It is not easy to wipe us out, we were
> Raised under the shade of swords
> And the crescent dagger is our national symbol (*Baang-e-Dara* 159)

As a children's poem and a national song this is much different from the modern national poems that are usually about the nation-state. The very first lines place the reader beyond the boundaries of a nation-state and connect with a trans-national heritage. The reader lays claim to China, and Arabia as well as Hindustan. This claim is justified under a Muslim identity: the only passport required to make such a claim. The rest of the verses contain an article of faith, a history of Muslim global encounters, and a universal symbol. A reader can claim the whole world as home because of his/her Muslim identity; the core tenet of this identity is *Tauhid*: Absolute faith in the oneness of God. This global community has faced times when the world has attempted to eliminate or subsume it, but that cannot be accomplished as this group of people is no stranger to warfare, and their symbol—the crescent moon—is but a curved dagger. So what brings this community together and gives it a universal sphere of feeling are its global reach, its history of suffering, its faith, and its martial prowess.

The poem was a reworking of an earlier poem, also a *tarana* that he had written for Indian children most probably in 1905. Titled *Hindustani Bachoon Ka Geet* (A Song for Indian Children) the poem is focused on Hindustan and contains a more composite form of nationalism. Iqbal's later poems lose this kind of composite nationalistic theme and focus primarily on the global Muslim identity. The main reason for this is Iqbal's philosophical interest in the universal nature of Islam and his distrust of the local politics of the Indian National Congress, especially since he had become an active member of the All-India Muslim League after the 1920s. Here are some verses from Iqbal's earlier poem:

> Where Chishti[16] announced his message of truth
> Where Nanak[17] sang the song of *Tauhid*
> What became finally the Tartar's home
> What made the Arabs leave their desert
> That is my *watan*, that is my *watan*. (*Baang-e-Dara* 87)

What makes this poem slightly limited and more oriented towards territorial nationalism is the last two lines above that serve as a refrain. This reference to *watan*, meaning territorial nation, is quite rare in Iqbal's work. The main spirit of the poem, however, is still Islamic: This is the land that witnessed one of the greatest Sufi saint's early missionary efforts and where Guru Nanak spread his message. What is instructive about this reference to Nanak is that despite being the founder of Sikhism, he transformed Hindu pantheism to the concept of *Tauhid*, giving an Islamic tinge to Hinduism. Similarly, India is the land that became home to the Tartars, famous for their itinerant way of life. Iqbal here is referring to the Mughal dynasty whose lineage went back to Mongol ancestors. The land also attracted a lot of Arab Sufis and as another verse in the poem indicates: 'The leader of Arabia had felt/the caress of a cool breeze from here' (87). This is a reference to particular *hadis* of the prophet who is believed to have said that he felt a cool breeze coming from Hind, which led the later Muslim scholars to believe that India was supposed to be the future abode of Islam. Both these poems can be read more acutely if read through Paul Brass's views on nationality-formation:

> The process of nationality-formation is one in which objective differences between peoples acquire subjective and symbolic significance, are translated into group consciousness, and become the basis for political demands. There are two stages in the development of a nationality. In the first stage, a particular group takes the leadership, attaches symbolic value to certain objective

characteristics of a group...and attempts to communicate that myth to the defined population.... The second stage in the formation of a nationality involves the articulation and acquisition of political rights for the group. (43-4)

I suggest that Paul Brass's theoretical explanation can be applied to these two poems of Iqbal. In my opinion Iqbal is not choosing certain random symbols but expressing his politics through the universal Islamic symbols already available to him. He has enhanced the significance of these symbols since they were poems for children. Two Islamic symbols the *crescent moon* and *tauhid* have been used in these *taranas*. *Tauhid*[18]contains universal significance for Muslims because it is a basic requirement for a person to qualify as a Muslim. Literally, when someone is converting to Islam, he has to recite the Arabic incantation *La Ilaha illallah Muhammad ar Rasulallah* (There is no God but Allah and the Muhammad is his Prophet). This declaration, called *Kalimat-ul-Tayyiba* (The cleansing utterance) is the incantation that cleanses, converts, and grants a person entry into Islam, an entry that cannot be blocked by any worldly power unless the person renounces this basic tenet of Islam. This symbolic value of the *Kalima* already exists in the Muslim consciousness. Iqbal only mobilizes it as a reminder and a didactic tool for his young audience. Through this symbol of *tauhid*, Iqbal is educating his young audience about the concept of a universal Islamic nation.

The second symbol in the first *tarana* is the crescent moon. Again, Iqbal need not attach any symbolic value to it; it already has universal Islamic symbolic value historically attached to it: the crescent moon heralds the beginning of each lunar month in the Islamic calendar, its replicas adorn the minarets of mosques, and its sight signifies several Islamic festivals. Making the moon analogous to the curved dagger—the Saracen scimitar—is where Iqbal uses his poetical license to connect the most enduring Muslim symbols within the Muslim mythology of resistance, action, and jihad. Read with such insights the *tarana* becomes a significant didactic tool to teach the nation, but this nation encompasses the Muslim universal, the *ummah* and not just a specific nation-state. Paul Brass's theoretical explanation does apply to Iqbal's poems, but the nation that is signified through this process is trans-historical and supranational. In comparison, both these *taranas*, one clearly pan-Islamic and the other slightly territorial, convey the way Islam is central to Iqbal's national expression.

As far as the Western territorial nationalism itself is concerned, Iqbal was militantly opposed to it. I will now briefly discuss one of Iqbal's most important poems, *Wataniat: Watan Behasiat aik Siasi Tasawwur Ke* (Nationalism: Country as a Political Concept) on the concept of territorial nationalism. To facilitate a better discussion, I will first provide a translation of some of its lines, and then discuss its salient features:

> Country is the greatest of new gods
> Its tunic is the shroud of religion
> This idol carved by the new civilization
> Is the destroyer of the Prophet's House
> You, whose hand is strengthened by *Tauhid*
> You Mustafwis[19] whose country is Islam
> Show this world a hidden sight
> And smite this idol into dust
> Being land-bound is destructive
> Live free like the fish in the sea
> Migration is the Prophet's *Sunnah*[20]
> You should bear witness to the truth:
> A country is something different in political words
> And something else in the Prophet's words.
> The friction amongst nations is because of it
> Trade aimed at conquest is because of it
> Politics without truth is because of it
> The destruction of the weak is because of it
> It divides God's people into nations
> It cuts the roots of Islamic nationhood. (*Baang-e-Dara* p. 60)

Iqbal's approach here is comparative. He is clearly juxtaposing the two competing principles of nation-forming: the Western nation-state model, and the Islamic concept of *ummah*. For him the Western model is akin to Ibn-e-Khaldoon's *asabiya*, which he terms *wataniat*. Both these concepts are similar because they invoke a particularly territorial and thus limited sentiment. For Iqbal, then, the concept of territorial nation-state is a major threat to the larger Muslim universal. I have already discussed Iqbal's views about the West, but this poem is an indictment of the flagship of Western political accomplishment: the Nation-State.

This emphasis on a pan-Islamic Muslim identity is strictly political, for the *ummah* by definition is the global Muslim community linked by law. Iqbal also draws upon the most enduring Islamic myth of *hijra* (migration). Based on the Prophet Muhammad's (PBUH) migration from Makkah to Madina, territorial loyalty cannot supersede the loyalty to the *ummah*, and if life becomes difficult in one's own territorial abode then one must, like the Prophet, leave for a place where one is able to live a life according to one's beliefs. There are several recorded sayings of the Prophet on the topic of *hijra*, which have been stressed upon in Islamic jurisprudence, and make it imperative on a Muslim to migrate in the name of God. A larger Muslim universal, therefore, is a necessity for a Muslim to exercise the option of migration. Iqbal's *tarana* also highlights one of the important principles of nation-forming: 'existence of other group(s) from whom the group is to be differentiated' (Brass 45). The creation of this other, Iqbal asserts, then becomes the means to rationalize the imperial nation-state's mercantile and exploitative drive. Against the divisions generated by the nation-state, Iqbal reasserts the idea of human unity. In another poem entitled 'Makkah or Geneva' Iqbal opines:

> In these times the nations have proliferated
> And the unity of Adam has been hidden
> The wisdom of the West is to divide the people
> Islam aims only at the nation of Adam
> Makkah sends this message to Geneva:
> Would it be Union of the People or Union of Nations? (519-20)

This unity is certainly political and transnational, for if it was only cultural, then there could be no threat to larger Muslim culture even if divided into nation-states. With such strong views against territorial nationalism, it is difficult to understand Iqbal's views on the future Muslim state of India, which he envisioned in his 1930 speech at the annual session of the All-India Muslim League, due to which he is revered as the national poet of Pakistan.

I shall discuss the dichotomy that exists between Iqbal the poet, and Iqbal the political visionary in the next chapter. It should suffice here to suggest that Iqbal displays the same kind of dual approach to modernity that most of the Islamic world faced as it entered Western modernity under colonialism. Al-Ahsan describes this feeling as follows:

> With the development of nationalism, and in particular the Muslim nation-state, the Muslims seem to have become somewhat confused about where their first loyalty lies—whether primary loyalty belongs to the *Ummah* or to the nation-state. (29)

Al-Ahsan here is referring to the postcolonial phase of Islamic nations. In Iqbal's case this anxiety was already a part of the elite consciousness. In my view, this schizoid view of the nation is inherently inscribed in the Muslim encounter with colonialism. As we have seen in almost all the literary works discussed above, the colonial encounter forces the native's to return to the pre-colonial universal myths. In case of Muslims this myth does not need to be invented, for it is present in their history, their daily rituals and cultural symbols. Since Iqbal takes it upon himself to speak to the people, he must then invoke the ideal historical symbol: the *ummah*. I, therefore, do not see these two competing claims of loyalty as Muslim confusion, but as a strength of political Islam: its power to keep its universal myth alive even after the long colonial encounter.

In Iqbal, then, we see a culmination of a long process of literary production. The writer's role that altered after the rebellion from esoteric Persian conventions to the question of political self-representation, as seen in Ghalib's poetry, has been transformed to that of a spokesman with an alternative political vision. In this process, we also saw Hali and Azad's loyalist emphasis along with a utilitarian emphasis of the production of literary texts, which was expressed in the novels of Nazeer Ahmad through the lives of his characters and their interaction with the British system. We also saw that not all literary production was loyalist and apologetic and that writers like Shibli Naumani and Akbar Allahabadi offered their own differing views on the build up of new power structures. Loyalism itself was, as we have seen, a political strategy initiated by the elite, but normalized in the name of the people, to create a space for the Muslims of India in the post-rebellion political and economic system. In Iqbal, then, the Muslim literary production dismantles the house of the master's ideas and offers its own reinvigorated world-view. In the political arena this emphasis is facilitated by the rising Muslim political consciousness, which has also undergone a transformation. From a question of winning special privileges for the Muslim masses in the British political and economic system, it has now shifted to the question of seeking a separate nation-state.

By Iqbal's time, then, the Muslim literary production had moved into what most theorists and historians consider a legitimate nationalist movement.[21] We have also learned in the process that this nationalist feeling and Muslim exceptionalism preceded party politics and was expressed in the works discussed above during all phases of the Muslim colonial experience.

NOTES

1. As a poet, Iqbal's work includes four volumes of Urdu verse and seven volumes of Persian poetry, a total of 1720 printed pages.
2. Some useful secondary books in Urdu about Iqbal's life and work include works by Ijazulhaq Quddusi, Muhammad Hanif Shahid, Sayyid Abdullah, and Abdul Majeed Salik.
3. A part of this chapter previously appeared *in The International Journal of Asian Philosophical Association* Vol. 1, No. 1 (2208) and is reproduced here with the permission of the editors.
4. Sir Thomas Arnold, in Hafeez Malik's words, was 'an accomplished scholar of Islam and modern philosophy. After teaching for almost ten years at the Anglo-Muhammadan College, Aligarh, Sir Thomas became professor of Philosophy at the Government College [Lahore] in February 1898' (12).
5. All citations from Khalifa Abdul Hakim's Urdu works are in my translation.
6. A good example of this is Iqbal's respect for Thomas Arnold to whom he dedicated his PhD dissertation.
7. In my translation.
8. *Afrangi* or *farangi* is the most frequently used Persian word for Europeans.
9. I have dealt with Iqbal's concept of the Muslim hero elsewhere in detail. See Raja 'Death as a Form...' in the Works Cited.
10. In the Sufi tradition *Qalandar* is the sort of mystic who is beyond material desires and does not depend on the material world for his sustenance.
11. *Iblees* is the Arabic term for Satan.
12. *Iblees* in Iqbal is always a dynamic character and not just represented as the evil Satan. He possesses all major qualities expected of human beings except obedience to God's will. He is, therefore, lost in the wilderness of his own making, but he is defiant and proud.
13. Iqbal uses the Persian term *Yad-e-baiza*, the glowing hand. In the Islamic tradition the glowing hand was one of the miracles of Moses, who, after an audience with God, raised his glowing hand as a testimony of God's confidence in him.
14. Cited in my translation.
15. The absolute belief in the oneness of God. The first precept of Islam.
16. A reference to Khwaja Mueen-ud-Deen Chishti, the founder of the Chishtia Order of Sufism and one of the early Muslim Sufis to bring Islam to India.
17. Guru Nanak, the founder of Sikhism, which is considered a synthesis of Islam and Hinduism.
18. I am using *Tauhid* as a symbol because of its symbolic significance. Just the word, when invoked, carries the signification of Muslim differences from all other religious communities. The Islamic nation is basically the nation of *Tauhid*, of people who must have absolute faith in the oneness of God. *Tauhid* is also important because its opposite concept, *Shirk* (creating an equal to God), is the only sin that, according to the Qur'an, God will not forgive.
19. Followers of the Prophet Muhammad (PBUH) who was also known as Mustafa.
20. The way of the Prophet.
21. For example, both John Breuilly and Bruce McCully date the rise of Indian Muslim nationalism to the party politics of the 1940s.

7

The Politics of Muslim Nationhood: Iqbal and Mawdudi

In the quest for nationhood, the burden of proof was obviously on the Muslims. While the Hindu leadership could draw upon the geographical, historical, and the popular precedence to forward a claim for a united, multiethnic India, the Muslim concept of the nation was always amorphous, arbitrary, and under constant revision. Any claim to a Muslim nationhood, therefore, was read as a descent into communalism. The Muslims themselves were not united in their quest for the secular ideal of a separate homeland, for the religious elite considered it an act of sundering the Muslim nation of India. Thus, while the Muslim League desperately needed the invocation of the nation to mobilize the public, it could only do so by highlighting inherent political tensions within the unionist concept of the nation. My discussion will now focus on Muhammad Iqbal and Abul A'ala Mawdudi's attempts at articulating the idea of a separate Muslim nation-state.

Iqbal was the first Muslim scholar and politician to delineate the physical boundaries of a future Muslim nation-sate in India. In his 1930 Presidential address at the Annual Session of the All-India Muslim League (AIML), Iqbal articulates a philosophical basis for a separate nationhood; and two years later, at the AIML Annual Conference of 1932, he articulates a more direct and precise method of creating separate Muslim homelands for the Muslims of India. Though a lot was being written during this time on the nature of Muslim national politics, these two speeches, being public in nature, are two extremely important articulations of the politics of Muslim nationhood and nation-state.

Both the speeches are quite different in their tone. While one is more didactic, the second one assumes a more declarative tone. By terming it as didactic, what I mean is that in this speech Iqbal attempts to define a need for a strictly Muslim nation-state in India. The second speech, by suggesting a possible geographical division of India, then, becomes a sort of declaration. In fact, during the first address, Iqbal apologizes for the 'apparently academic discussion' (*Muslim Political* 195). He attempts to answer the following questions in his first speech:

> What, then, is the problem and its implications? Is religion a private affair? Would you like to see Islam, as a moral and political ideal, meeting the same fate in the world of Islam as Christianity has already met in Europe? Is it possible to retain Islam as an ethical ideal and to reject it as a polity in favour of national polities, in which religious attitude is not permitted to play any part? This question becomes of special importance in India where the Muslims happen to be in a minority. (196)

All these questions stem from Iqbal's deeply Islamic worldview. And his ideas about Islam and its juxtaposition with the fate of European Christianity are quite instructive, for Iqbal clearly posits that it was the concept of the nation-state that destroyed the universal appeal of Christianity. Hence, the question puts the future of Islam within the larger historical context of its competing world religion, Christianity. For Islam to succeed in India as a socio-political system, a separate nation-state is necessary, and that is why for Iqbal what fractured the Christian universal is not likely to happen to Islam as long as the Muslims remember that Islam is a complete code of life and not only a matter of individual faith and belief. And since only in a purely secular conception of the Indian nation would Islam become a private affair, it is, therefore, imperative on the Muslims of India to have their own autonomous regions where Islam can function as a normative socio-political system.

Iqbal goes on to speculate that, 'if the Indian Muslim is entitled to a full and free development on the lines of his own culture and tradition in his own Indian home-lands…, he will be ready to stake his all for the freedom of India'(199). It is important to note that this claim of the contingency of Muslim participation in the freedom struggle, only if the Muslims are promised their own autonomous homelands, is a natural outgrowth of Muslim exceptionalism as discussed previously. Unlike the Hindu majority, Iqbal suggests the Muslim opposition to the British and their union with the Hindus will be conditional to the demands of their particular nation-state.[1] In his speech Iqbal also highlights his own vision of a future Muslim Indian state, which forms a blueprint for the future demand for Pakistan:

> I would like to see the Punjab, North-West Frontier Province, Sind and Baluchistan amalgamated into a single state. Self-government within the British

Empire or without the British Empire, the formation of a consolidated North-West Indian Muslim State appears to me to be the final destiny of the Muslims. At least of North-West India. (200)

Within the context of Indian politics of the time, this is the most concrete articulation of a Muslim nation-state; it revolutionizes Muslim politics of freedom, for now what would be a future Pakistan is no longer an abstract concept but a feasible reality. Iqbal does not suggest this as the only solution, but rather as a final option if the Muslims do not want to abandon the dynamic claims of Islam as a way of life in favour of a secular nation-state in which religion is a private affair.

In his second speech, Iqbal is even more confident of his vision and completely aware of the prevailing charged political climate on the question of Muslim nationhood. He begins by putting forward his own idea of nationhood as opposed to the Western concept:

Politics have their roots in the spiritual life of man. It is my belief that Islam is not a matter of private opinion. It is a society, or if you like, a civic church. It is because present-day political ideals...may affect its original structure and character that I find myself interested in politics. I am opposed to nationalism as it is understood in Europe...I am opposed to it because I see in it the germs of atheistic materialism, which I look upon as the greatest danger to modern humanity. Patriotism is a perfectly natural virtue and has a place in moral life of man. Yet that which really matters is a man's faith, his culture, his historical tradition. These are the things which, in my eyes, are worth living and dying for, and not the piece of earth with which the spirit of man happens to be temporarily associated. (211-12)

To Iqbal, thus, Islam is by nature political and cannot be declared only as a private affair; being a Muslim means being in the world. The idea of a Muslim nation, therefore, is only sustainable if it is forwarded in the interest of creating a free Islamic society, for this is what really matters, rather than simply territorial affiliation. Hence, territorial nationalism will only mean something for a Muslim if it promises a system of life and politics guided by the principles of Islam. Iqbal goes on to highlight the nature of Muslim–Hindu demands, how both these opposing groups look at the nature of nationhood:

The majority community pretends to believe in a nationalism theoretically correct, if we start from Western premises, belied by facts if we look to India. Thus the real parties to the present struggle in India are not England and India, but the majority community and the minorities of India, which can ill-afford to accept the principle of Western democracy until it is properly modified to suit the actual conditions of life in India. (214)

Of course, the majority here are the Hindus and the minority are the Muslim community. This minority community, the Muslims, Iqbal contends, has a wholly different world-view than the one posited by Western political thought. It is this aspect of the Muslim world-view that Iqbal mobilizes to build up a case for a separate Muslim homeland in India. It is important to note that Iqbal is quite consistent in his articulation of the Muslim nation. In all of his Urdu poetry he has never supported nationalism in its purely Western form. To him nationalism for the Muslims of India cannot simply be an end in itself; it must also be a means at accomplishing an autonomous territory in which Muslims are able to live according to the precepts of their own religion. And since the religion of Islam, according to Iqbal, besides being spiritual in context, is also political in nature, hence, this expression of spirituality is presented in a clear concept of nation.

Besides these two speeches and a few private letters, Iqbal does not offer much in terms of his articulations of a future Muslim nation-state. Several other literary personalities, of whom Abu'l A'ala Mawdudi is probably the most prominent and influential exponent of a separate Muslim nation-state, take up this particular task.

Mawdudi was 'born on 25 September 1903...in Awrangabad, Deccan, the youngest of...five children (Nasr 9). Raised in a deeply religious family, Mawdudi received a sound early education in matters of faith, but instead of following his brothers in working towards a strictly religious profession, Mawdudi, from a very early age, dreamed of becoming a writer.' (Nasr 9-14). Thus, through journalistic experimentation, and through his own observations of writing styles, Mawdudi, according to Vali Nasr, was able to develop an original style of writing in Urdu; a style more accessible for the common reader. Nasr records Mawdudi's thoughts on the process of writing in the following words:

> I believe that every thought has its own vocabulary, and each thought has to be expressed in the proper balance of words. Therefore, I believe it is enough to choose the right words, and there is no need for unnecessary entanglements. I was able to economize on writing and to devote most of my time to gathering information, evidence, and sources for my thoughts. Having ordered my thoughts in my mind, transferring to paper does not require much. (14)

Thus, in Mawdudi we finally see a colonial Muslim subject who feels impelled to write, and whose writing, geared towards a Muslim audience, is avowedly simple and easy to understand. Another important aspect of Mawdudi's influence in the public debates on the Indian Muslims is the inherent political nature of his times, for Mawdudi's 'intellectual awakening occurred in tandem with his increasing interest in politics and his participation in the independence movement' (Nasr 15). Thus, by the time Mawdudi enters the public arena, the idea of separate nationhood for Indian Muslims, having matured as a viable concept, has become almost axiomatic, and the main quest of the elite is to popularize this national identity to the majority of the Muslim populace. In Mawdudi's case, the task is further facilitated by the accessibility of his language and the immediacy of his conversation with the masses: almost all his works are published as occasional pieces in his journal *Tarjuman-Al-Qur'an*. Using some of his works dealing with the question of Muslim–British relations, and his views on the question of Muslim nationhood, I would now attempt to explore the significance of Mawdudi's textual production during the last decade of the Pakistan Movement.

As a respected religious scholar, Mawdudi, thus, becomes a prominent voice of Muslim particularism, Muslim revivalism, and eventually of the demand for a separate Muslim homeland. I will now briefly touch upon Mawdudi's 1937 essays on the subject of Muslim nationhood[2] with the backdrop of attempts by the Indian National Congress to sway Muslims to their side.[3]

Mawdudi begins by elaborating upon the key political objectives of the Muslim freedom struggle, which in his view, 'is the kind of freedom which ensures that not only would Islam remain in India, but would also become a prestigious and powerful force' (67). Thus, from the outset it is clear that for Mawdudi any nationalist movement that weakens the role of Islam in Muslim political life, and replaces it with 'nation-worship' (67) is completely unacceptable. If the Muslim political objective is on these lines, then the next step is to define and organize their politics around it. Mawdudi then goes on to explain the dual nature of Muslim nationhood in India, which according to him, inhabits two contemporaneous subjectivities:

> Two conditions prevail in India: that of Hindustanis and that of Muslims. In our first condition we share the same plight as that of other nations of this country... But for the second condition our problems are completely related to us. And no other nation shares it with us. (75)

This is one more articulation of Muslim exceptionalism, but it has now found a different voice and a larger popular audience. Mawdudi's sundering of the Muslim identity in two now proposes a politics different from the politics of Unionist Nationalism, for the Muslims can only be successful if both aspects of their political identity are accommodated. If the Muslims have to alter or abandon their Muslim identity in order to forge a nationalistic alliance, then that, according to Mawdudi, is absolutely impossible. Mawdudi then goes on to challenge the Hinduized Western concept of nationhood:

> Those who want us to follow the path of nationhood only as Hindustanis follow the Western concept of nationhood, which has the Hindu view of humanity deeply embedded in it. They aim to eliminate the national differences caused by religious and traditional differences and replace them by one nation united under the mixture of Hinduism and communism...We can only follow this path if we sacrifice our second condition of nationality, our Muslimhood. (76-7)

Hence, any compromise that limits Islam as being the private affair of the individual and not as a complete political system, to Mawdudi, is an unacceptable compromise. What is important to note here is that like Iqbal, Mawdudi too believes that Islam cannot be simply reduced to the private sphere, and encompasses a complete way of life, including the public and political. Hence, even at this earlier stage of the Muslim freedom movement, the debate is the same; the refusal to accept religion as simply the private affair of the individual. A nationalism that precludes the possibility of making Islam a possible source of guiding the public sphere cannot be acceptable. Hence, this makes the demand for a separate nation imperative on the Muslims.

In another essay,[4] 'Does India's Salvation Lie in Nationalism?' published in 1939 and included in the same compilation, Mawdudi attempts to answer this nationalist question with a reference to the Western concept of nationhood and in opposition to some Muslim attempts made at Unionist Nationalism. For Mawdudi the main difference between 'Western Nationalism' and 'Spiritual Nationalism'[5] is that, 'spiritual nationalism connects people through ethical and spiritual relationships and creates a larger human cooperation, while nationalism and ethnic difference sever these connections, and replace human companionship with strife and enmity' (351). As Islam, according to Mawdudi, has been and must aspire to be a world system, it cannot follow the territorial and ethnic model of nationhood. Mawdudi then goes on to explain the possibilities of creating Indian nationalism. He explores the possibilities of creating a single nation out of various traditional ethnicities in a country. In his view, under the prevailing circumstances, only two possibilities can exist:

1. One ethnic civilization conquers the others.
2. A combined civilization is created through the integration of all different ethnic nations. (365)

Mawdudi suggests that the first possibility does not apply to India, but he dwells at length on the second possibility. For the integration model he opines: 'it cannot be built in one or two days, but needs centuries for it to be nourished' (365-6). According to Mawdudi, this kind of national integration is not possible in India and he stipulates his reasons as follows:

> These nations have much deeper differences as compared to the ethnic nationalities of Europe. They have different religions; their rules of civilization are completely different. Their rules of conduct and sources of tradition are also completely different and incommensurate....Here we cannot forge one nation in the name of political and economic interest alone. Unfortunately, the one hundred and fifty years of British rule has completely weakened the national character of these nations....Under such circumstances, nation building, which would further demolish the already weakened national fibre, is unthinkable and would lead to drastic consequences. (369)

Mawdudi clearly suggests that to launch a new project of Unionist Nationalism is not only unacceptable at a religious level but is also not feasible pragmatically. For him, both Hindus and Muslims lack the time and the vigour to embark on such a monumental project of building a nation based on one single tradition, as they both also happen to be from two separate traditions. Hence, it seems, the Muslims of India must look for an alternative to the integrative model. And as Mawdudi has already pointed out the bare essentials of a Muslim nationhood, and the need for the role of Islam in the public sphere, it cannot simply be a nation in which Muslims are a large minority with some privileges afforded under the family law as a separate group of people. What this points out is the necessity of a sovereign Muslim nation-state. To forward a detailed answer to the problems of Muslim nationhood, Mawdudi publishes three suggestions in 1938:

First Sketch

To create a democratic state in a country containing two or more nations, the following must be ensured: First, it should be based on rules of international federation, or in other words a state of federated nations; Two, each nation that forms a part of this federation must have complete cultural autonomy; Third, the combined national activities of this state must be based on equal partnership. (485-6)

Second Sketch

If the international federation is not acceptable, then different nations should be given different territories where they can create their own democratic nation-states. They should be given approximately twenty-five years to accomplish the exchange of populations. In such conditions we would be willing to make a federated state with the non-Muslims. (491-2)

Third Sketch

Our separate nation-states should be formed, and they should have their own separate federation. Similarly, the Hindus should have their own federation, and then these two separate nations can have a sort of loose confederation. (492)

It is important to note that by the time Mawdudi puts forward these three possible solutions to the problems of Indian nationhood, he has already proven that the Muslims do constitute a separate nation and that they inhabit a dual identity: that of Indians and Muslims contemporaneously. Hence, all these solutions are based on this basic premise about Muslim identity. As pointed out earlier, it is also important to remember that Mawdudi's complex ideas are presented in everyday Urdu and are very accessible through their publication in *Tarjuman-Al-Qur'an*. Thus, from the very beginning, Mawdudi's intervention in the debates about Muslim nationalism is immediate and public. Also included in the second volume of *Muslims and the Indian Freedom Movement* is an academic paper by Mawdudi presented by him in 1940 at the Aligarh Muslim University. This paper, titled 'How Can an Islamic Government be Established', provides further details of Mawdudi's thoughts on the subject. Having discussed the nature of Muslim national identity in his earlier works, Mawdudi has, by this time, narrowed his focus in defining the lineaments of an eventual Muslim state. Before providing an explanation of the constituent elements of an Islamic state, Mawdudi first describes the process through which a group of people—in this case the Muslims of India—will reach a certain critical stage in developing an Islamic nation; his emphasis on gradualism is important to note here. Mawdudi writes:[6]

> I am not suggesting a deterministic approach to governmentality, an approach that completely elides human will, but what I am suggesting is that just deciding to form a certain kind of government is not enough. To create the desired form of government, one must first provide the material structures that make it imperative to eventually form the kind of government that is needed.... Thus, when people have struggled for a long time and have reached a time when any system of government not suitable for their temperament can succeed, then and only then, a natural system of government emerges that mirrors the struggles of the people. Thus, you will notice that a good government emerges only when there is a confluence of popular action, good leadership, individual character, collective character, and a common plan. (162)

Thus, for Mawdudi the establishment of an Islamic government is an organic and natural process and cannot be forced through revolution. The material conditions for its creation must be first created, and in the case of India, creating a separate Muslim homeland is one such basic step. Unlike the secular leaders of the All-India Muslim League, for Mawdudi, Islam is not simply a mobilizing ideology, but rather, the whole purpose of demanding a separate homeland for the Muslims of India is a first step in creating a truly Islamic state. Mawdudi also provides two basic constituents of an Islamic state: 'The Islamic state is ideological and is based on the idea of divine sovereignty'[7] (167). By an 'ideological state' what Mawdudi means is a state based on an ideological identity, and not defined by other markers of national identity such as ethnicity, language, or culture. By defining the Islamic state as ideological, Mawdudi hopes to accomplish a greater degree of national unity. In his view, 'The idea of an ideological government does not see different *qaums* but just human beings, who are offered an ideological system of government. Those who accept this ideological system, become equal partners in governing the state' (166). Thus, simply stated, while Mawdudi's Islamic government does not discriminate on the basis of race, language, culture, or colour, it will, however, in the end, include only those as equals who believe in the state ideology, and as state ideology is based on Islam, the state would, thus, automatically become an Islamic state. It is not difficult to guess that in such a definition of a state, while minority rights are protected by the state, they however, are never given equality of status, as in Mawdudi's terms, they have not met the basic requirements of accepting the ideological definition of the state.

While Iqbal resorted to the premise of the concept of God's ownership of the earth as an equalizing principle, for Mawdudi, the acceptance of this basic principle is the cornerstone of a future Islamic state. He explains his concept of divine sovereignty:

> The second important characteristic of an Islamic state is that its entire edifice is built around the idea of divine sovereignty. Its basic premise is this: the country belongs to God and He alone is its true ruler. No individual, group, or nation has the right to sovereignty. Only God has the right to promulgate laws and issue commands. Man is only God's vice-regent on earth, and may only rule within the laws provided by God. (168)

Thus, not only is the Islamic state ideological and based on a religious and metaphysical explanation of reality; it must also be governed in the name of God. This second stipulation ensures that any future Muslim state will not be Islamic in name only, but it will also be Islamic in its day-to-day functioning through the adoption of the Shariah as their body of laws. And new laws will be evolved with the guidance of the Shariah. Certainly, this narrow definition of the future Islamic nation clashed with the political agenda of All-India Muslim league, for whom, as I stated earlier, Islam was a mobilizing ideology but not necessarily the core guiding system for the future Muslim nation-state. In fact, in the case of Jinnah it is historically evident that he had envisioned a liberal, secular model for a future Muslim nation-state. It is imperative to note that by the mid-forties Mawdudi's Jamaat-i-Islami had also evolved into a viable political force, and their long-term political agenda was at variance with the All-India Muslim League. In another essay of the same collection published in 1945, Mawdudi, while responding to a reader's question, provides the reader with the following reasons for his party's abstention from electoral politics:

> You should understand the nature of our party's stance on current electoral politics. As a principled political party, it is impossible for us to compromise our basic principles. Our main fight with the current regime is based on this simple difference of opinion: this system is based on the principle of 'sovereignty of the people'. In opposition to this, we believe that sovereignty does not belong to the people, but to God.... So, if we are true to our beliefs, then we must stake our whole in fighting for the simple principle of divine sovereignty, and for as long as this principle is not accepted, we cannot participate in the elections. (227-8)

This is how the narrative of Indian Muslim nationhood finds different expressions. While the early exponents of the Muslim cause desperately needed to create a space for the Muslims within the hegemonic project of the empire, during the terminal stages of the freedom struggle, one important strand of national struggle is focused primarily on cleansing the Muslim consciousness of the residual effects of the hegemonic negotiation of the Western system. Both Iqbal and Mawdudi represent the struggles of two such reformers in retrieving and articulating a Muslim identity separate from the Hindus but also in difference to the in identity-forming imperatives of the British hegemonic project.

Iqbal and Mawdudi are both aware of the pitfalls of purely Western secular nationalism and are skeptical about it. For them Islam must form the basis of everyday life in an Islamic state and must not be reduced to the affair of the individual. It is this public nature of Islam as a way of life that forces the Muslim scholars of this particular path, for there were dissenting views, to makes it imperative for the Muslims to seek a separate, autonomous nation-state. Hence, while Iqbal articulates a grand vision of the nation, Mawdudi, highly influenced by Iqbal but also the more conservative of the two, illustrates the tactical details of the Muslim nationalistic vision. Together they generate an elite and popular discussion that is later appropriated by the Muslim League in its quest for a separate nation-state for the Muslims of India. Eventually, while Jinnah and the All-India Muslim League use Islam as a marker of national difference and as a mobilizing ideology, the followers of Mawdudi, on the other hand, consider Islam the very basis of a separate Muslim nation-state. This difference in imagining the role of religion in a future Muslim nation-state, as we now know in hindsight, would come to define the very basis of the normalizing struggles of the future Muslim nation-state.

NOTES

1. Mawdudi later picks up on this particular insight and builds his case for a distinctly separate Muslim concept of nationhood, which I discuss later.
2. All citations from this particular Urdu text are in my translation. For details see Mawdudi, *Tehrik*.
3. Mawdudi's *magnum opus* on the Muslim concept of nation and nation-state *Islami Riasat* [The Islamic State].
4. This essay was published in 1939. For details see Mawdudi, *Therik* 335-377.
5. Mawdudi uses the term *Ilahi Shariat*, which literally means God's Law, for the term is a compound of two Arabic words *Ilaha* and *Shariah* (God and Law). I have roughly translated it as 'Spiritual Nationalism' which in this particular instance means a sense

of nationhood based on a solidarity created under the rules of one particular religion and its system of law.

6. All citations from Mawdudi's paper are in my translation.

7. Mawdudi's term for this is *Kilafat-e-Ilahiyya*, which literally means God's government.

Conclusion

On 23 March 1940, the leaders of the All-India Muslim League, led by Mohammad Ali Jinnah, gathered in Lahore and passed a resolution in favour of an independent Muslim nation-state. The resolution came to be known as the Pakistan Resolution. The name Pakistan was not mentioned in the resolution: the naming followed the resolution and has generated its own mythologies. The main clause of the resolution demanded:

> Resolved that it is the considered view of this Session of the All-India Muslim League that no constitutional plan would be workable in this country or acceptable to the Muslims unless it is designated on the following basic principle, viz. that geographically contiguous units are demarcated into regions which should be so constituted with such territorial adjustments as may be necessary, that the areas in which the Muslims are numerically in a majority as in North-western and Eastern Zones of India should be grouped to constitute 'Independent States' in which the Constituent Units shall be autonomous and sovereign. (Quoted in Ambedkar 9)

For Jinnah and the Muslim League, the next seven years were years of intense activity. There were several counter resolutions, including one passed by the Jamiat-ul-Ulama-e-Hind, the political party affiliated with the Deoband scholars opposed to the creation of Pakistan. From 1940 to 1946, several major lengthy works were written on Pakistan, including one written by B.R. Ambedkar, another by Rajendra Prasad, and yet another by F.K. Khan Durrani. It seemed that everyone held an opinion either in favour of the idea of Pakistan or against it.

On 14 August 1947, both India and Pakistan won their freedom from the British as two sovereign nation-states. The division of India precipitated the largest cross-border migration of people in modern history. And while the British Empire absolved itself of any further responsibility to the people of India and Pakistan, the two newly formed nations also experienced unspeakable atrocities committed on both sides of the national divide. The Partition did not only create two separate nation-states, it also caused two separate national ideologies and narratives of mutual distrust and belligerency. This part of history, at least, is well recorded and normalised within the national narratives of post-independence India and Pakistan. Thus, in the official historiography of these two nations the division of India came to signify both, a tragedy and a triumph, respectively. While 23 March is now celebrated in Pakistan as the Pakistan Resolution Day and all other alternate visions have been eliminated from Pakistani historiography, 23 March 1940 has also become an important date for the historians and scholars of Pakistani nationalism, for they all consider it the official initiation of Pakistani nationalism.

I began this book with a reference to Mohammad Ali Jinnah's inaugural speech as the first Governor-General of Pakistan. The subsequent pages of my inquiry into the creation of Pakistan have been an attempt at re-reading the textual history of the Pakistan Movement to suggest that the moment of independence so gratefully celebrated by Jinnah in his first speech was made possible by a prolonged, and often complex, discourse of the Muslim national identity. My attempt, mostly conducted through close readings of chosen texts of the Muslim nation of India, is also an effort to overwrite the conventional explanations of the creation of Pakistan on both sides of the postcolonial national divide of the Indian subcontinent. Thus, Pakistan was neither an outcome of a British conspiracy, as portrayed in the Indian departmental view, nor caused by irreconcilable differences between Hindus and Muslims as posited in the departmental history of postcolonial Pakistan under the general rubric of the 'Two Nation Theory'. In a traditional reading of history, the quest for Pakistan is traced only through the politics of the Muslim League after 1940, and the creation of Pakistan is inextricably linked with the spectre of Muslim communalism. Yet, the Muslims of India could not have been so easily misled by the so-called communal politics of the All-India Muslim League or, for that matter, intransigence of Mr Jinnah. Therefore, in my reading of Indian Muslim history, I have attempted to suggest that the idea of Muslim separateness and exceptionalism took shape in the works of poets, scholars, and political leaders long before party politics became a popular phenomenon. In such a reading, Indian Muslim nationalism precedes the party politics of both the Indian National Congress and the All-India Muslim League. It is such reading of Indian Muslim history that can inform a more enriching scholarship for the past, present, and future of Pakistan.

I do not claim this to be an exhaustive or all encompassing inquiry with a definitive explanation for the creation of Pakistan. A single book, I believe, cannot explain the complex processes, leadership choices, and popular actions that underwrite any freedom struggle. What I have attempted, however, is a re-reading of some canonical and some forgotten texts to suggest that the idea of Muslim separateness and exceptionalism took shape immediately after the 1857 Rebellion due to drastic alteration of Muslim material conditions. My discussion of what I have called the 'Foundational Texts' is, therefore, an attempt at proving this point. How far this effort has been successful will be, as always, decided by my audience, for the true value of a text is always in the hands of its readers.

Pakistan is a nation of over one hundred and sixty million people, and it has, like so many other postcolonial nations, struggled to produce, articulate, and popularise its normative structures. Due to its strategic location, its recent problematic role as a regional US ally in the war against terror, and its national potential as a leading Muslim nuclear power, Pakistan is one of the most important Muslim nation-states of the twenty-first century. Unfortunately, since the terrorist attacks of 2001, Pakistan has been mostly represented as a problem both in the media as well as in the scholarly works produced in the United States. Thus, I hope that my attempt at articulating the formative national history of Pakistan will facilitate a more engaged public debate and academic scholarship on the past, the present, and the future of Pakistan.

Works Cited

Abdul Hakim, Khalifa. *Fikr-e-Iqbal* (Iqbal's Thought). Lahore: Bazm-e-Iqbal, 1988.

————. *Islam and Communism.* 1951. Lahore, Institute of Islamic Culture, 1969.

Abdullah, Sayyid. *Vali se Iqbal Tak.* (From Vali to Iqbal). Lahore: Maktaba Khyban, 1976.

Ahmad, Aijaz. 'Jameson's Rhetoric of Otherness and the "National Allegory".' *Social Text,* No. 17 (1987): 3-25.

Ahmad, Aziz. *Islamic Modernism in India and Pakistan: 1857–1964.* London: Oxford University Press, 1967.

Ahmad, Nazeer. *Mirat-ul-Urus.* (A Bride's Mirror), 1869. *Majmua Deputy Nazeer Ahmad.* (Collected Works) Ed. Salim Akhtar. Lahore: Sang-e-Meel, 2004.

————. *Ibnulwaqt.* (The Time Server), 1888. *Majmua Deputy Nazeer Ahmad.* (Collected Works) Ed. Salim Akhtar. Lahore: Sang-e-Meel, 2004.

————. *Mu'za-e-Hasnah.* (Collected Letters). Ed. Iftikhar A. Siddiqui. Lahore: Majlis-e-Taraqi Adab, 1963.

Ahmad, Tufail Sayyid. *Musslamanoon ka Roshan Mustaqbil* (The Bright Future of the Muslims). Delhi: Kutubkhana-e-Azizia, 1945.

Akhtar, Ahmad Mian. *Iqbaliat ka Tanqidi Jaiza.* (A Critical Review of Iqbaliat). Lahore: Iqbal Acadmy, 1955.

Akhtar, Saleem. *Urdu Adab ki Mukhstar Tareen Tarikh.* (The Shortest History of Urdu Literature). 20th Edition. Lahore, Pakistan: Sang-e-Meel, 2000.

Al-Ahsan, Abdullah. *Ummah or Nation: Identity Crisis in Contemporary Muslim Society.* Leicester: The Islamic Foundation, 1992.

Ambedkar, B.R. *Pakistan or the Partition of India.* 1945. http://www.Columbia.edu/itc/mealac/Pritchett/00ambedkar. 17 April 2009.

Anderson, Benedict. *Imagined Communities,* 1983. Revised Edition. London: Verso, 1991.

Batalwi, Subhan Rai. *Khulasatat Tawarikh.* Lahore: Urdu Science Board, 2002.

Bhabha, Homi K. ed. *Nation and Narration.* 1990. New York: Routledge, 2004.

Brass, Paul R. *Language, Religion, and Politics in North India.* 1974. Lincoln: iUniverse, 2005.

Chakrabarty, Dipesh. *Provincializing Europe: Postcolonial Thought and Historical Difference,* Princeton: Princeton University Press, 2000.

Chatterjee, Partha. *The Nation and its Fragments.* New Jersey: Princeton University Press, 1993.

Chaudhuri, S.B. *Civil Rebellion in the Indian Mutinies, 1857–1859.* Calcutta, 1957.

Chinweizu. *Towards the Decolonization of African Literature.* New York: Taylor and Francis, 1998.

Deutsch, Karl. 'Nationalism and Social Communication.' *Nationalism.* Eds. John Hutchinson and Anthony D. Smith. New York: Oxford, 1994.

Duff, Alexander Rev. *The Indian Rebellion: Its Causes and Results.* New York: Robert Carter and Brothers, 1858.

Durrani, F.K. Khan. *The Making of Pakistan.* Lahore: Sh. Muhammad Ashraf Publishers, 1944.

Fanon, Frantz. *The Wretched of the Earth*. Trans. Constance Farrington. New York: Grove Press, 1963.

Faruqi, Ziya-ul-Hassan. *The Deoband School and Demand for Pakistan*. New York: Asia Publishing House, 1963.

Fatehpuri, Farman. *Pakistan Movement and Hindi–Urdu Conflict*. Lahore: Sang-e-Meel, 1987.

Ghalib, Assadullah Khan. *Dastanbuy: A Diary of Indian Revolt of 1857*. 1858. Translated by Khwaja Ahmad Farooqi. New York: Asia Publishing House, 1970.

————. *Ghalib Ke Khatut*. (Letters of Ghalib). Ed. Khaliq Anjum. Five Volumes. New Delhi: Ghalib Institute, 2000.

Gramsci, Antonio. *Selections from the Prison Notebooks*. Trans. and Eds. Quintin Hoare and Geoffrey Smith. New York: International Publishers, 1971.

Guha, Ranjit. *Subaltern Studies I*. New Delhi: Oxford UP, 1982.

————. 'Dominance Without Hegemony and its Historiography.' *Subaltern Studies VI*. 1989. New Delhi: Oxford UP, 1994.

Hali, Altaf Husain. *Musaddas-e-Hali*. 1875. Lahore, Pakistan: Khazeena-e-Ilmo Adab, 2004.

————. *Muqaddama-e-She'r-o-Shairi*. (An Introduction to Poetry). 1893. Ed. Dr Waheed Qureshi. Lahore, Pakistan: Maktaba-e-Jadeed, 1953.

————. *Hayat-i-Javed: A Biography of Sir Sayyid*. 1901. Trans. David J. Mathews. New Delhi: Rupa & Co, 1994.

Hamza. El. *Pakistan: A Nation*. Lahore: Sh. Muhammad Ashraf Publishers, 1941.

Hardy, P. 'Ghalib and the British', *Ghalib: The Poet and His Age*. Ed. Ralph Russell. New Delhi: Oxford University Press, 1997.

Hasanul Lughat: Farsi–Urdu (Persian–Urdu Dictionary). Lahore: Oriental Book Society, 1997.

Hibbert, Christopher. *The Great Mutiny: India 1857*. 1978. New York: Penguin, 1980.

Hunter, W.W. *The Indian Musalmans*. 1871. Third Edition. Calcutta: Comrade Publishers, 1945.

Hussain, Iqbal. 'Akbar Allahabadi and National Politics.' *Social Scientist*, No. 180 (May 1988): 29-45.

Ikram, Sheikh Muhammad. *Rud-e-Kausar*. 1957. Lahore: Adara-e-Saqafat-e-Islamia, 2003.

————. *Mauj-e-Kausar*. 1962 Lahore: Adara-e-Saqafat-e-Islamia, 2003.

Iqbal, Muhammad. *Baang-e-Dara*. 1924. *Kulyat-e-Iqbal* (Iqbal's Collected Works: Urdu), Lahore: Mahmood Siddiqullah, 1972.

————. *The Reconstruction of Religious Thought in Islam*. 1930. Lahore: Sang-e-Meel, 1996.

————. *Muslim Political Thought: A Reconstruction*. Ed. Fateh Muhammad Malik. Lahore: Alhamra, 2002.

————. *Baal-e-Jibreel*. 1935. *Kulyat-e-Iqbal*: (Iqbal's Collected Works: Urdu). Lahore: Mahmood Siddiqullah, 1972.

————. A Message from the East. (*Payam-e-Mashriq*). 1922. Trans. M. Hadi Hussain. Second Edition. Lahore: Iqbal Academy, 1977.

————. *Armughan-e-Hijaz*. 1938. *Kulyat-e-Iqbal*: Urdu (Iqbal's Collected Works: Urdu). Lahore: Mahmood Siddiqullah, 1972.

Jalal, Ayesha. *The Sole Spokesman: Jinnah, the Muslim League and the Demand for Pakistan*. New York: Cambridge University Press, 1983.

————. *Javid Nama* (The Pilgrimage of Eternity). 1932. Trans. Shaikh Mahmoud Ahmad. Lahore: Institute of Islamic Culture.

Jalibi, Jamil. 'Akbar Allahbadi: *Aik Bunyadi Baat.* (Akbar Allahbadi: A Basic Point). http://www.urdustan.com/mazameen/akbar_jalbi.html, Visited 19 February 2009.

Jameson, Fredric. 'Third-World Literature in the Era of Multinational Capitalism.' *Social Text,* No. 15 (1986): 65-88.

———. *Postmodernism: Or the Cultural Logic of Late Capitalism.* Durham: Duke University Press, 2001.

Khan, Badsha. *My Life and Struggle.* Trans. Helen B. Bouman. Ed. K.B. Narang. Delhi: Hind Pocket Books, 1969.

Khan, Sayyid Ahmad Sir. *Asbab-e-Baghawat-e-Hind.* 1859. (Causes of the Indian Revolt). Trans. G.F. Graham and Auckland Colvin, 1873. Ed. Salimuddin Qureshi. Lahore: Sang-e-Meel, 1997.

———. *Writings and Speeches of Sir Sayed Ahmad Khan.* Ed. Shan Muhamad. Bombay: Nachiketa Publications, 1972.

Lavan, Spencer. 'The Kanpur Mosque Incident of 1913: The North Indian Muslim Press and its reaction to Community Crisis.' *Journal of the American Academy of Religion,* Vol. 42, No. 2 (Jun. 1974): 263-79.

Lelyveld, David. *Aligarh's First Generation: Muslim Solidarity in British India.* Lahore: Book Traders, 1991.

Lipner, Julius J. Ed. and Translator. 'Introduction' *Anandamath or the Sacred Brotherhood.* Bankimcandra Chatterji. 1880. New York: Oxford University Press, 2005.

Macaulay, Thomas Babington. 'Minute on Indian Education', *Postcolonialism.* Eds. Gaurav Desai and Supriya Nair. New Burnswick: Rutgers University Press, 2005, 121-31.

Malik, Hafeez and Lynda P. Malik. 'The Life of the Poet Philosopher', *Iqbal: Poet Philosopher of Pakistan.* Ed. Hafeez Malik. New York: Columbia University Press, 1971.

Mawdudi, Abul A'la. *Tehrik-e-Azadi-e-Hind aur Musalman* (Muslims and the Indian Freedom Movement), Vol 1,1937. Lahore: Pan-Islamic Publishers, 1976.

———. *Tehrik-e-Azadi-e-Hind aur Musalman* (Muslims and the Indian Freedom Movement), Vol. 2, 1937. Lahore: Pan-Islamic Publishers, 1976.

———. *Islami Riasat* (The Islamic State). 1967. Lahore, Pakistan: Islamic Publications, 2000.

Mehr, Ghulam Rasul. *Sayyid Ahmad Shahid.* Lahore: Kitab Manzil, 1952.

Metcalf, Barbara. *Islamic Revival in British India: Deoband, 1860–1900.* New Jersey: Princeton University Press, 1982.

Muhammad, Shan. *Sir Syed Ahmad Khan: A Political Biography.* Meerut: Meenakashi Prakashan, 1969.

Munawwar, Muhammad. *Dimensions of Pakistan Movement.* Rawalpindi: Services Book Club, 1993.

Naumani, Shibli Maulana. *Kulyat-e-Shibli*: Urdu (Urdu Collected Works of Shibli). Ed. Sayyid Suleman Nadwi. Islamabad: National Book Foundation, 1989.

———. *Maqalat-e-Shibli* (Essays of Shibli), Vol. 5, Ed. Sayyid Suleman Nadwi. Islamabad: National Book Foundation, 1989.

———. *Maqalat-e-Shibli* (Essays of Shibli), Vol. 8, Ed. Sayyid Suleman Nadwi. Islamabad: National Book Foundation, 1989.

———. *Sirat-ul-Nabi* (Life of the Prophet), Vol. 1, 1917. Lahore: Maktaba-e-Madina, 2001.

Nasr, Seyyed Vali Reza. *Mawdudi and the Making of Islamic Revivalism,* New York: Oxford University Press, 1996.

Noble, David. *Death of a Nation: American Culture and the End of Exceptionalism,* Minneapolis: University of Minnesota Press, 2002.

Parsad, Rajendra. *India Divided,* 1946. Third Edition. Bombay: Hind Kitabs, 1947.

Pritchett, Francis. *Nets of Awareness: Urdu Poetry and its Critics*. Berkeley: University of California Press, 1994.

Punjabi, A. *Confederacy of India*. Lahore: Nawab Muhammad Shah Nawaz Khan of Mamdot, 1939.

Quddusi, Ijazulhaq. *Iqbal aur Ulama-e-Pak-o-Hind*. (Iqbal and Ulama of India and Pakistan). Lahore: Iqbal Academy, 1977.

Raja, Masood Ashraf. 'Death as a Form of Becoming: The Muslim Imagery of Death and Necropolitcs.'*Digest of Middle East Studies* Vol. 14, No. 14 (2005): 11-26.

———. 'Muhammad Iqbal: Islam, the West, and the Quest for a Modern Muslim Identity'. *The International Journal of Asian Philosophical Association*. Vol. 1, No. 1, 2008: 33-45.

Rahman, Fazlur. *Islam and Modernity: Transformation of an Intellectual Tradition*. Chicago: University of Chicago Press, 1982.

Renan, Ernest. 'What is a Nation' Trans. Martin Thom. *Nation and Narration*. Ed. Homi Bhabha. New York: Routledge, 1990.

Robinson, Francis. 'Technology and Religious Change: Islam and the Impact of Print'. *Modern Asian Studies*, Vol. 27, No. 1 (Feb. 1993): 229-51.

Russell, Ralph. Ed. *Ghalib: The Poet and his Age*. New Delhi: Oxford University Press, 1997.

———. *The Seeing Eye: Selections from the Urdu and Persian Ghazals of Ghalib*. Lahore: Alhamra, 2003.

Said, Edward. *The World, the Text, and the Critic*. Cambridge: Harvard University Press, 1983.

———. *Humanism and Democratic Criticism*. New York: Palgrave/Macmillan, 2004.

Sadiq, Muhammad. *A History of Urdu Literature*. Delhi: Oxford University Press, 1964.

Salik, Abdul Majeed. *Zikr-e-Iqbal*. Lahore: Bazm-e-Iqbal, 1983.

Saran, P. Dr. *The Provincial Government of the Mughals: 1525–1658*. 1941. Lahore: Faran Academy, 1976.

Schimmel, Annemarie. *Islam in the Indian Subcontinent*. Lahore: Sang-e-Meel, 1980.

Shah, Sayed Wiqar Ali. *Ethnicity, Islam, and Nationalism*. Karachi: Oxford University Press, 1999.

Shahid, Muhammad Haneef. Ed. *Nazr-e-Iqbal*. Lahore: Bazm-e-Iqbal, 1972.

Sharpe, Jenny. *Allegories of Empire: The Figure of Woman in the Colonial Text*, Minneapolis: University of Minnesota Press, 1993.

Smith, Anthony D. 'The Crisis of Dual Legitimation', *Nationalism*. Eds. John Hutchinson and Anthony D. Smith. New York: Oxford, 1994.

———. *National Identity*. Las Vegas: University of Nevada Press, 1991.

Spear, Percival. 'Ghalib's Delhi' *Ghalib: The Poet and His Age*. Ed. Ralph Russell. New Delhi: Oxford University Press, 1997.

Suleri, Sara. *The Rhetoric of English India*. Chicago: University of Chicago Press, 1992.

Thanesari, M. Ja'far. *Kala Pani*. (Black Water), 1879. Ed. Muhammad Sarwar Tariq. Faisalabad: Tariq Academy, 2004.

Thanewi, Maulana Ashraf Ali. *Beheshti Zewar* (Ornaments of Heaven), 1927. Lahore: Kutab Khana-e-Jamili, 2005.

Varma, Pavan K. *Ghalib: The Man, the Times*. New York: Penguin, 1989.

Vishwanathan, Gauri. *Masks of Conquest: Literary Study and British Rule in India*. New York: Columbia University Press, 1989.

Watt, Ian. *The Rise of the Novel*, Berkeley: University of California Press, 1957.

Zaidi, Ali Jawad. *A History of Urdu Literature*, Delhi: Sahitya Akademi, 1993.

Index